NEW YORK Food Crawls

Ali Zweben Imber & Daryl Zweben Hom
The Sisterhood of the Unbuttoning Pants

TOURING *the* **NEIGHBORHOODS**
ONE BITE & LIBATION *at a* **TIME**

Globe Pequot
GUILFORD, CONNECTICUT

Globe
Pequot

An imprint of The Rowman & Littlefield Publishing Group, Inc.
4501 Forbes Blvd., Ste. 200
Lanham, MD 20706
www.rowman.com

Distributed by NATIONAL BOOK NETWORK

Copyright © 2018 Ali Zweben Imber and Daryl Zweben Hom

Maps: Melissa Baker © The Rowman & Littlefield Publishing Group, Inc.

British Library Cataloguing in Publication Information available
Library of Congress Cataloging-in-Publication Data available

Names: Imber, Ali Zweben, author. | Hom, Daryl Zweben, author.
Title: New York City food crawls : touring the neighborhoods one bite
  and libation at a time / Ali Zweben Imber & Daryl Zweben Hom, The
  Sisterhood of the Unbuttoning Pants.
Description: Guilford, Connecticut : Globe Pequot, [2018] | Includes
  index. | Identifiers: LCCN 2018024471 (print) | LCCN 2018025314
  (ebook) | ISBN 9781493035922 (e-book) | ISBN 9781493035915
  (pbk. : alk. paper) | ISBN 9781493035922 (ebook)
Subjects: LCSH: Restaurants—New York (State)—New York—Guidebooks.
Classification: LCC TX907.3.N72 (ebook) | LCC TX907.3.N72 N4437 2018
  (print) | DDC 641.59747/1—dc23
LC record available at https://lccn.loc.gov/2018024471

♾™ The paper used in this publication meets the minimum requirements
of American National Standard for Information Sciences—Permanence of
Paper for Printed Library Materials, ANSI/NISO Z39.48-1992

Printed in the United States of America

Contents

Introduction

OUR LIVES IN NEW YORK CITY HAVE ALWAYS REVOLVED AROUND FOOD: eating it, writing about it, talking about it, then eating it some more. . . . We believe that the best way to take a bite out of the Big Apple is to dive in and have all buttons bursting, and we have eaten our way through the boroughs, exploring exotic cuisines, undiscovered gems, and some of the top restaurants in the world. In a city with seemingly endless options for a good meal, we hope this book helps to open your eyes and bellies to new culinary experiences.

Follow the Icons

 If you eat something outrageous and don't take a photo for Instagram, did you really eat it? These restaurants feature dishes that are Instagram famous. These items must be seen (and snapped) to be believed, and luckily they taste as good as they look!

 Cheers to a fabulous night out in New York City! These spots add a little glam to your grub and are perfect for marking a special occasion.

 Follow this icon when you're crawling for cocktails. This symbol points out the establishments that are best known for their great drinks. The food never fails here, but make sure to come thirsty, too!

 This icon means that sweet treats are ahead. Bring your sweet tooth to these spots for dessert first (or second, or third).

THE UPPER EAST SIDE CRAWL

1. **AMARANTH,** 21 E. 62ND ST., NEW YORK, (212) 980-6700, AMARANTHRESTAURANT.COM

2. **FRED'S AT BARNEYS MADISON AVENUE,** 660 MADISON AVE., NEW YORK, (212) 833-2200, WWW.BARNEYS.COM

3. **SERAFINA ALWAYS,** 33 E. 61ST ST., NEW YORK, (212) 702-9898, SERAFINARESTAURANT.COM

4. **E.A.T.,** 1064 MADISON AVE., NEW YORK, (212) 772-0022

5. **SERENDIPITY III,** 225 E. 60TH ST., NEW YORK, (212) 838-8531, SERENDIPITY3.COM

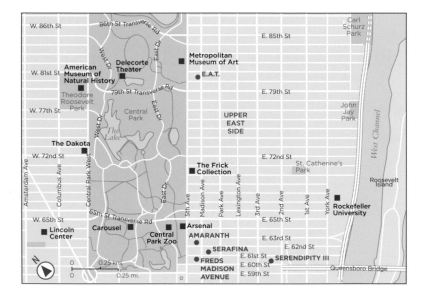

Upper East Side

Where to Go for Food Amid the Fashion

A TRIP TO NEW YORK CITY IS NOT COMPLETE WITHOUT PROPER RETAIL EXPLORATION ALONG MADISON AVENUE, but if a blood sugar–induced dressing room meltdown is not on the menu, a meal should figure prominently into every shopping outing. Deciding which pair of black boots to buy is hard enough without the added pressure of figuring out where to eat, and a little planning will save your energy for those really important decisions. Carbs and couture generally don't mix, so we recommend planning ahead, trying on the most size-sensitive items before lunch, and saving the tipsy afternoon purchases for accessories. If you are more Giacometti than Givenchy, these restaurants are also in close proximity to many major museums, such as the Metropolitan Museum of Art, the Met Breuer, and the Guggenheim.

1

AMARANTH

AMARANTH is ground zero for ladies who lunch professionally, with air-kissing staff and a menu designed for small waistlines and large wallets. This the quintessential uptown eatery, with smartly dressed men and women making up the lunch scene, nannies and children in early evening, and sophisticated locals at night. The staff is always nicer to faces that they recognize, but mere mortals can have a pleasant time by making a reservation and not expecting a table up front. The slightly cramped quarters recall a bistro in Paris, but the vibe is classic Upper East Side. The menu at Amaranth is accessible and varied, with enough options so that regulars can dine several times a week and not get bored, and the staff is used to accommodating dietary requests, be they for health or personal preference. Everything is excellently prepared and fresh; the cold poached salmon will keep you in your smaller size, and the focaccia is always good for a splurge.

2 FRED'S AT BARNEYS MADISON AVENUE

Take the elevator directly to the top floor of Barneys—do not stop for shoes on floor five, do not head to the basement for beauty products, just put your blinders on, get in that elevator and head up as high as you can. You can work off your lunch later by taking the escalator down and walking the floors, making **FRED'S** Italian fare relatively guilt-free. Unless you want to strategically jockey for a seat at the bar, reservations are essential during prime times, and even though you might still have to wait a bit, it will make the whole experience much more pleasant. Service at Fred's is passable at best, but the food makes up for it; be dainty and get the famous Mark's Madison Avenue salad with Italian tuna, or be indulgent and get our favorite dish, the Emilia Romagna pizza, which features Parmesan and aged balsamic vinegar. The prices at Fred's are not for the faint of heart, but compared to everything else at Barney's, they are a relative bargain.

3 SERAFINA ALWAYS

SERAFINA ALWAYS has built a mini-empire on Italian food so good it attracts scores of visiting Europeans in addition to locals. The signature yellow awnings are a beacon of hope after a long day of pounding the pavement, promising comforting food and a full bar. A large menu of salads, pastas, thin-crust pizzas and heartier specialties makes it a no-brainer for grabbing a bite when the fashion fatigue sets in. A favorite dish is the Focaccia di Sofia, a homemade focaccia stuffed with creamy robiola and truffle oil, perfect for sharing (or not). The Stoli pasta will warm you up and fill you with creamy, vodka-sauce happiness. There are several locations throughout the Upper East Side, and you can always expect equal numbers of strollers and stilettos.

4 E.A.T.

Restaurateur and grocer Eli Zabar knows the Upper East Side, and this unassuming dining room attached to the retail outlet of the same name is the go-to for titans of industry who need their morning bagel and schmear. A perfect spot for solo dining after a visit to the Met, **E.A.T.** serves elevated comfort food; think tomato soup full of bright acid and firm chunks of bread, juicy brisket sandwiches, and of course the famous bagel and smoked fish tower. For the indecisive, a wide variety of cold salads are available in any combination, including the addicting lentils vinaigrette. It is futile to resist picking up a pastry on the way out, and the shop also has suitable options for a last-minute hostess gift, as well as premade sandwiches if you want to take your bites to go.

5 SERENDIPITY III

Fueling sugar rushes for over 60 years, **SERENDIPITY III** is all about good old-fashioned, high-calorie fun; so if shopping is your cardio, this is your reward. The can't-miss item that keeps customers lining up is the Frrrozen Hot Chocolate, a decadent rite of passage for any kid (or adult) in New York City. The savory part of the menu is composed of indulgent, made up diner fare, and the sweets are served on a monstrous scale, as if created by Willy Wonka himself. The decor is whimsical, featuring colorful Tiffany lamps and charm that evokes old-school soda shops.

THE UPPER WEST SIDE CRAWL

1. **BARNEY GREENGRASS,** 541 AMSTERDAM AVE., NEW YORK, (212) 724-4707, BARNEYGREENGRASS.COM

2. **WHITE GOLD BUTCHERS,** 375 AMSTERDAM AVE., NEW YORK, (212) 362-8731, WHITEGOLDBUTCHERS.COM

3. **GRAY'S PAPAYA,** 2090 BROADWAY, NEW YORK, (212) 799-0243, GRAYSPAPAYANYC.COM

4. **LEVAIN,** 351 AMSTERDAM AVE., NEW YORK, (212) 874-6080, LEVAINBAKERY.COM

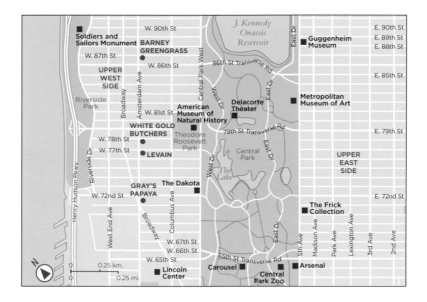

Upper West Side

Old-School Treats and New-School Eats

THE UPPER WEST SIDE IS HISTORICALLY REGARDED AS THE INTELLECTUAL, BOHEMIAN SIBLING OF THE BLUE-BLOODED UPPER EAST SIDE, a neighborhood hard to define but heavily influenced by its proximity to Columbia University, the Museum of Natural History, and Lincoln Center. Stately brownstones and gothic high-rises located mere blocks from both the park and the river make the Upper West Side appealing to families, and night-life is more likely to involve a trip to the ballet than dancing on banquettes, which also means more mommies than millennials. Speaking of moms, mom-and-pop shops are still a part of the fabric of the neighborhood, an increasingly rare asset these days. The Upper West Side has an authentic mix of restaurants that have survived the changes in the neighborhood by staying true to themselves and offering a side of sentimental value, as well as newer, artisanal options.

1

BARNEY GREENGRASS

Talk about a Super-Nova! There is nothing more New York than breakfast (or any meal really) at **BARNEY GREENGRASS**. The "Sturgeon King" has been selling top-notch smoked fish and spreads since 1908, in its present location since 1929, and although it may seem that the dining room has not had a refresh since opening day, it is all part of its charm. The throngs of families waiting for hours on weekends and the devoted regulars who pop in for breakfast daily are more concerned with smoked salmon and sable than the scene. Barney Greengrass's old-school practices can seem like shtick, but if you have been around that long there is no time for shtick; the waiters are on the curt side of chatty and quick with a quip. The retail portion can be chaotic and cash is preferred at certain times, but it is a charming sort of chaos. The smoked fish dishes eclipse the meats and salads; the scrambled eggs with lox and sable could convert a nun and one bite of any fish on a bagel with cream cheese will have you looking to buy an apartment around the corner, it's just that good.

WHITE GOLD BUTCHERS

WHITE GOLD is in great juxtaposition to Barney Greengrass; they also serve classic sandwiches and dishes, but with locally sourced, niche ingredients and a price tag to match. The farm-to-table ethos and hipster attitude of the staff makes it seems like it should be worlds away from Barney Greengrass, not just mere blocks. Like Barney Greengrass, White Gold Butchers also offers a

retail portion and restaurant, but their wares are boutique mustards and hot sauces, in addition to the butchered-on-premise meats. The bacon egg and cheese is a fancy upgrade from the bodega standard, and their version of a chopped cheese features all-organic, grass-fed beef and pickles; the chicken has a yellow tint because the chickens were fed marigolds, and so on. White Gold is a place in the neighborhood, but not necessarily a neighborhood place.

3

GRAY'S PAPAYA

The typical idea of a New York City hot dog is a dirty-water dog hastily consumed in a moment of pure desperation, mustard dripping from your mouth onto a tissue-thin napkin, but real New Yorkers know a better way to get their frankfurter fix. **GRAY'S PAPAYA** has been synonymous with hot dog heaven since it opened in 1973, offering all-beef hot dogs and tropical juice drinks every hour of the day, every day of the year; and yes, that means breakfast hot dog sandwiches. The commitment to the 24/7/365 is genuine; there are no locks on the door and no light switches, because they literally never close.

The menu has been the same since their opening, and many of the employees have been there for over 30 years. A "New York Style" hot dog means covered in sauerkraut and their special onion sauce, and the Recession Special is two dogs and a fruit drink (or soda) for $4.95, which is probably less than anything from a cart near Central Park.

4 LEVAIN

LEVAIN opened in 1994, but its attention to detail and small-batch nature feel very modern and of the moment. Their mission is simple: make the best chocolate chip cookie. Although Levain has several outposts, it still feels very local, with an authentic and straightforward commitment to making people happy. The signature cookie is a wonder, an actual feat of science that is massive, crispy, and firm on the outside and cooked perfectly gooey and raw on the inside, with semisweet chocolate chips and walnuts. Levain's appeal is obvious, and its popularity well earned, and as the cookies have become more and more famous, they have installed a Cookie Line Cam, so potential customers can judge the line before showing up. Levain has become a destination, but is also very much a neighborhood place, with locals showing up for baguettes and scones, if they can resist the cookies.

THE MIDTOWN CRAWL

1. **THE BAR AT LE BERNARDIN,** 155 W. 51ST ST., NEW YORK, (212) 554-1515, LE-BERNARDIN.COM

2. **SUSHI YASUDA,** 204 E. 43RD ST., NEW YORK, (212) 972-1001, YASUDA.COM

3. **21 CLUB,** 21 W. 52ND ST., NEW YORK, (212) 582-7200, 21CLUB.COM

4. **THE GRILL,** 99 E. 52ND ST., NEW YORK, (212) 375-9001, THEGRILLNEWYORK.COM

5. **CASA LEVER,** 390 PARK AVE., NEW YORK, (212) 888-2700, CASALEVER.COM

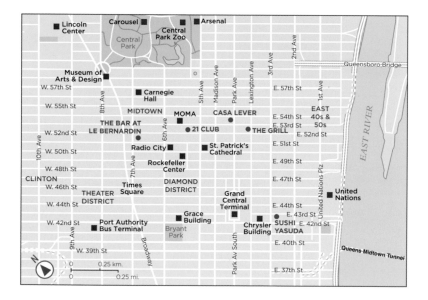

Midtown

Where to Eat on an Expense Account

MIDTOWN IS A PURE INJECTION OF BIG-CITY ADRENALINE, an instant crash course in Essential New York City 101. Many of the iconic images associated with the Big Apple are found in this part of town; gleaming skyscrapers, luxury shopping meccas with intricate window displays, grand old-school hotels, the horse-drawn carriages in Central Park, and of course pushy people rushing down the sidewalks, exasperated by the slower pace of visitors. Due to its proximity to many big-money business headquarters, as well as the ritzy co-ops of the UES and UWS, much of the finest, dearest dining in the city is in this area. Whether you are dining on your own dime or your company's (even better), Midtown is the perfect spot to spoil yourself with a fancy meal from some of the best chefs in the world. You will return home lighter in wallet if not weight, but vacation calories don't count. . . .

1

THE BAR AT LE BERNARDIN

LE BERNARDIN is the best restaurant in Manhattan. That is a fact. Kitchen magician and overall swoon-inducing human Eric Ripert has a deft touch for preparing, dressing, and pairing all things seafood, as well as everything else. Le Bernardin is the fine-dining paradigm against which all others should be judged, in terms of the decor, the service, the plating and presentation, as well as Aldo Sohm's wine list. If the desire is to experience Le Bernardin without reserving a month in advance, or before or after another meal, the first-come-first-served seating in the bar/lounge area is an excellent option. Although available in the dining room if you

ask, the bar menu offers one of the greatest dishes of all time: the Le Bernardin Croque Monsieur—creamy toast squares filled with smoked salmon, swiss cheese, and caviar, this dish is both luxurious and simple, a revelation for your taste buds. N.B.: Across the courtyard is Aldo Sohm Wine Bar, offering amazing pours by the glass and the bottle, as well as tasty bar bites in a lively setting.

SUSHI YASUDA

Another temple to the proper service of fish, **SUSHI YASUDA** serves only pure, authentic sushi. While maki rolls are available, the best way to experience Yasuda is to sit at the counter and order *omakase*, leaving your fish fate in the hands of the masters. Although Yasuda himself has gone back to Japan, his staff is extremely skilled with a knife. Prices can add up, especially if there is boozing involved, but they also offer a killer deal at lunchtime. A few tips when eating *omakase*: Eat the fish as the chef serves it, quickly and in one bite if possible; do not drench the nigiri in soy sauce unless you are instructed to do so by the chef. If using soy sauce, dip the fish side in (rather than the rice), and never put your wasabi in the soy sauce and mix it around. Also, even though this is the finest sushi available, feel free to eat with your hands; it's an accepted way to enjoy sushi.

21 CLUB

The **21 CLUB** (or just "21" if you want to sound like a local) is a rich spot; rich in history, rich in flavor, and full of rich tabs. To go to 21 is to feel like you are being let in on a secret to which all true New Yorkers are privy. Secrets are actually a large part of the history of the 21 Club; remnants of its storied beginnings as a speakeasy can still be found in the legendary hidden wine room. There is a story for just about everything you encounter, including

the jockeys out front and the seemingly endless, whimsical toys hanging from the ceiling in the dining room. There are also certain tables that are associated with celebrities, so if you are with the Chairman of the Board, you might get lucky and get Sinatra's table.

The clubby, old-school, elegant vibe is enforced by the dress code, which still mandates jackets for men. The servers are all professionals, and dressed up as well, enhancing the rich sense of tradition. A martini at the bar is an easy way to get the 21 experience, as long as you peek into the dining room. The food is American and pretty straightforward, including chicken hash and a fantastic burger; there is something to be said for eating with your hands in such a special place. Also, not to be missed are the *pommes soufflées*, puffed but hollow potato crisps that look like an out-of-this-world science experiment. All meals should end with a chocolate soufflé, which is of course very rich.

4 THE GRILL

Don't let the name fool you—there is nothing backyard BBQ about this grill. **THE GRILL** is the hot spot in New York City, having recently undergone a major facelift, like the grand dame that she is. The Grill is one of the most iconic dining rooms in New York City, and in its former incarnation as the Four Seasons earned a reputation as the premier power spot for lunch, regularly hosting titans of industry, royals, and politicians. The glam factor is in full effect at The Grill, with socialites and celebrities making it hard for mere mortals to land a reservation at a respectable dinner time, but never has dining at 5:30 pm been so worth it. The dining room oozes old-school charm and luxury, complete with tuxedo-clad servers on hand to help navigate the menu of modified steak house standards. The wow factor takes full effect with the *pasta à la presse*, a dish that is not so much served as performed, with the sauce literally pressed tableside in a piece of equipment from the early 1900s, a duck press made in France and found in New Orleans. The prime rib is also a big show, arriving in a proper domed gueridon and carved into a large, juicy, meaty chunk right in front of salivating diners. Even the most carb-phobic would be challenged to resist the bread basket served at The Grill. If a reservation is hard to land, a drink or bite at the bar under Richard Lippold's sculpture and a glance at the famous dancing curtains is always an option to get a big dose of glamour with little planning.

5

CASA LEVER

For a dash of Italian style on Park Avenue, **CASA LEVER** is the spot. More Armani suits than Versace T-shirts, Casa Lever is an elegant restaurant that serves fresh, well-executed Italian food in a posh environment that is conducive to sealing the deal, whether professionally or personally, if you know what we mean. The front bar is lively and beautiful, and in the warmer months the outside lounge is the ideal spot to grab an Aperol spritz and loosen your tie over some bar bites, including truffle grilled cheese that will make you weep for your nonna, it's so good. Twirling pasta under the watchful gaze of Warhols on the wall is always fun, and Casa Lever does not take itself too seriously, with professional service that is never pretentious. For a side of culture with your carbs, the building for which the restaurant is named is an attraction in its own right; The Lever House was the first glass-and-steel building on Park Avenue, and its construction marked a turning point for American architecture. The building's lobby houses an art gallery with rotating exhibits of contemporary and modern art that are open to the public.

THE THEATER DISTRICT CRAWL

1. **SUSHI OF GARI 46,** 347 W. 46TH ST., NEW YORK, (212) 957-0046, SUSHIOFGARI.COM/RESTAURANTS/46TH

2. **IPPUDO WESTSIDE,** 321 W. 51ST ST., NEW YORK, (212) 974-2500, IPPUDONY.COM

3. **DB BISTRO MODERNE,** 55 W. 44TH ST., NEW YORK, (212) 391-2400, DBBISTRO.COM

4. **DANJI,** 346 W. 52ND ST., NEW YORK, (212) 586-2680, DANJINYC.COM

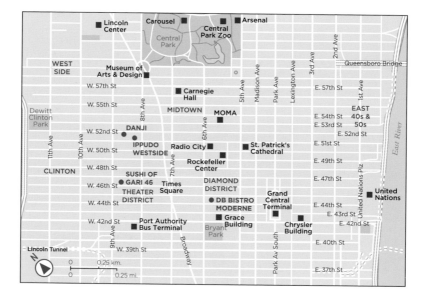

Theater District

How to Pre/Post with the Most

THE TIMES SQUARE THEATER DISTRICT AREA can be a tourist trap, but don't let the lights distract you from your mission; you will make your way through the life-size Elmos and past the Olive Garden and seek out proper New York City dining experiences. The Crossroads of the World is a nuisance for those who live and work in New York City, but going to see a play is an acceptable reason to spend time in the area, one of the few. You don't want to eat so much that you will be incapacitated by intermission, but you don't want to be shelling out for Junior Mints either, unless that is your thing, so there is no shame in eating both before and after your play.

1

SUSHI OF GARI 46

Sitting down for the *omakase* at **SUSHI OF GARI** is a show in and of itself, each piece presented individually as you patiently wait to see what the next act will bring. Leave ample time before your curtain, surrender yourself to the chef's whims, and be prepared to pay more than face value for the experience. At Gari the fish is given the royal treatment, dressed up, dressed down, and paired with the most interesting ingredients in order to elicit maximum flavor. Some of the pieces are striking in their simplicity and freshness, and other pieces will impress you with their inventiveness, such as raw salmon with stewed tomatoes. You will be awestruck as piece after perfect piece is presented to you—glistening tuna topped with tofu sauce and hot sesame oil; delicately seared cod; chopped eel and avocado that tastes like a dessert; sweet shrimp topped with a briny caviar treat; snapper topped with salad and a crispy lotus chip . . . and so on and so on. There is simple sushi available at Sushi of Gari, but it is truly a waste to bring a California roll–eating friend here. The atmosphere hovers somewhere between grim and bleak, but the fish more than makes up for it.

2 IPPUDO WESTSIDE

IPPUDO is the perfect post-theater stop to slurp ramen and dish about the show. Ippudo is always busy and often the waits can seem scary, even if post-show gives you better odds, so be prepared to be patient and try to get a drink at the bar. You will feel like a Broadway star walking into the two dining rooms, as the staff shouts out a greeting to every new guest. The ideal meal at Ippudo starts with buns: melt-in-your-mouth pork buns or the slightly naughty fried chicken buns. The buns have lettuce for crunch and mayo for mayo's sake, making them different from any other bun you might have. All of the ramen is perfection, especially the Akamaru Modern (served in the red bowl) which is full of garlicky, porky richness and will have you begging for an encore.

3 DB BISTRO MODERNE

If you are heading to a matinee, or want to make a pre/post-theater meal more of an event, then **DB BISTRO** is the right spot. Refined and elegant without being stuffy, db bistro serves updated French bistro classics and is an easier way to sample some of Daniel Boulud's renowned cuisine. There is a $55 pre-theater prix-fixe menu offered nightly that will have you fed well and on to your next activity in a timely manner; given Boulud's status as a top toque, this deal can't be beat. What also can't be beat is the famous db burger, a show-stopper/heartstopper stuffed with wine-braised short ribs and foie gras that essentially started the gourmet burger craze 17 years ago. db bistro is an oasis of gracefulness amid the hustle and bustle of the area.

4 DANJI

DANJI is a chill spot, serving inspired Korean food in a minimalist environment that feels intimate and energized. The kitchen is open late, and they play good tunes, making it ideal for post-play provisions. The menu is meant for sharing and features innovative interpretations of traditional Korean flavors and ingredients; Think beef *bulgogi* sliders, spicy "KFC'" Korean fire chicken wings, and bacon wet kimchi fried rice. Danji is destination dining, so seeing a play is just a good excuse to be in the neighborhood.

THE GRAMERCY/FLATIRON CRAWL

1. **GRAMERCY TAVERN,** 42 E. 20TH ST., NEW YORK, (212) 477-0777, GRAMERCYTAVERN.COM

2. **ABC KITCHEN,** 35 E. 18TH ST., NEW YORK, (212) 475-4829, ABCKITCHENNYC.COM

3. **SHAKE SHACK,** SOUTHEAST CORNER OF MADISON SQUARE PARK (NEAR MADISON AND 23RD ST.), NEW YORK, (212) 889-6600, SHAKESHACK.COM/LOCATION/MADISON-SQUARE-PARK

4. **UNION SQUARE CAFÉ,** 101 E. 19TH ST., NEW YORK, (212) 243-4020, UNIONSQUARECAFE.COM

5. **ELEVEN MADISON PARK,** 11 MADISON AVE., NEW YORK, (212) 889-0905, ELEVENMADISONPARK.COM

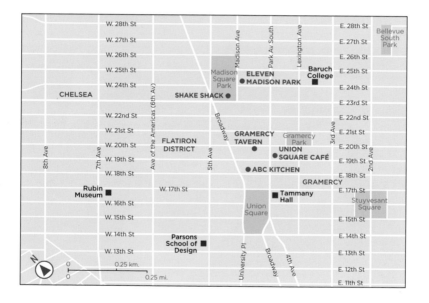

Gramercy / Flatiron

The Essential Foodie Crawl

MORE COVETED THAN AN HERMES BIRKIN BAG, a key to Gramercy Park has long been a status symbol for fashionable New Yorkers. The gated park, two idyllic acres surrounded by beautiful residential buildings and the iconic/infamous Gramercy Park Hotel, is only accessible to Gramercy Park residents, who are given an actual key. New Yorkers love nothing more than a venue that is hard to get into, and Gramercy Park is no exception; there is no doorman to tip or PR person to shmooze, so the only way in remains to buy an apartment, which is quite a lot of green to pay for access to a little swath of green.

Almost as hard to get into are the many top-tier, famous restaurants in Gramercy Park and the adjacent Flatiron District (named for the distinguished, oft-photographed profile of the Flatiron building on 23rd Street). These areas are unmatched in top chefs per block, making it a virtual red light district for indulging foodie fantasies. Reservations at certain spots should be procured as soon as a trip is booked in order to ensure availability at prime times, and Eleven Madison Park may cost more than your hotel room, but everybody knows that a few extra pounds and foodie bragging rights make the best souvenirs.

1

GRAMERCY TAVERN

GRAMERCY TAVERN is considered one of the best restaurants in New York City, and with good reason; every element of dining at Gramercy Tavern feels special, from the seasonal decor, to the attentive and proactive service, to the perfectly executed American food. There are two options for dining at "Gram Tav": the front "tavern room," which is only for walk-ins, and the proper dining room in the back, which only offers price-fixed and tasting menus for dinner, and a la carte dining for lunch. Wait times for both can be immense; reservations for the dining room are hard to come by, even after 24 years of business, and the tavern can run a wait for tables and bar seats of a few hours. A little planning is worth it to experience Chef Michael Anthony's cuisine. The food is composed but rustic, always seasonal, and manages to feel exciting and familiar at the same time. Gramercy Tavern is equally appropriate for a celebration, or just to make any day feel special.

2 ABC KITCHEN

ABC is so named for its location in the famous ABC Carpet and Home building, a huge maze of floors that sells some of the best furniture, linens, and knickknacks all under one roof. It is quite possible to enter ABC looking for one item and not leave until three days later, lots of money lighter and still missing the one item you originally went in for, but it is quite an impressive spot. Aside from sectional sofa, ABC Kitchen is its own destination, a Jean-Georges Vongerichten concept focusing on farm-to-table food in an open and airy setting all made from reclaimed items. All of the vendors are listed on the menu, and every dish feels fresh and bright, since only items that are in season will be served. ABC Kitchen is open for brunch, lunch, and dinner, and makes a perfect spot for a midday shopping break or early evening fuel-up. Standout dishes include the crab toast, the lobster, and the burger. Although always busy, it is possible to eat at the bar, and the front area is reserved for walk-ins. There are also two other dining options in ABC Home, both from Jean-Georges: ABC Cucina and ABC V.

3

SHAKE SHACK

The burger that built an empire, the original **SHAKE SHACK** in Madison Square Park is not to be missed. Although not quite a "shack," the only seating is on the tables and benches in the surrounding Madison Square Park, and there can be long lines at any time of the day. In addition to the Shack Burger and crinkle fries, Shake Shack makes a mean breakfast sandwich and offers some truly naughty sweets. Shake Shack is no longer unique to New York City: If you fly into Kennedy airport, you can grab a burger from a Shake Shack there as well, but there is something to be said for trying the burger where it all began.

4 UNION SQUARE CAFÉ

UNION SQUARE CAFÉ helped define the Union Square neighborhood when it opened on 16th Street in 1985. Perhaps it did too good of a job attracting people to the area because rising rents forced the original USC to shutter in 2015 and find a new home elsewhere. Now located on 19th Street, the revamped location retains its Union Square soul and menu staples, but in a much bigger space. The decor is evocative of the original, and there is still a large bar that is a perfect perch from which to sample the dishes and service that define Danny Meyer's style. The menu is hard to generalize; it has Italian elements as well as a farm-to-table feel. The pastas are consistently satisfying, authentic in their rustic execution. Union Square Café is not a restaurant tied to its location, but rather to how it makes you feel, which is most likely full and happy. Even with more room than before, Union Square Café can still run a wait to be seated, even with reservations. N.B.: Daily Provisions, also from USHG and located next door, has pastries, coffee, and sandwiches, as well as an excellent roast chicken in the afternoon.

ELEVEN MADISON PARK

ELEVEN MADISON PARK was recently recognized as the number-one restaurant in the world by The World's 50 Best Restaurants, and it also completed a total overhaul of their dining room and kitchen. Eleven Madison Park is the paradigm of what modern fine dining in New York City is; it is luxe without pretension, precise without stiffness, and exciting without excess. The menu changes seasonally, and the tasting menu is quite pricey, but there is no better way to spend a day. The servers are dressed formally but in grays rather than severe black tuxes, and all of the staff comes across as young and motivated, attentive without hovering, and are a refreshing departure from stiff formal service. The room has an Art Deco feel, featuring pops of

color against a muted palette, high ceilings and a wall of windows, which flood the space with light during the day. Although the menu changes, you can count on dishes with exciting twists that show extreme skill and lots of thought, and custom tableware and accessories bearing the restaurant's logo. Certain dishes have an accompanying story, and this and other touches come off as clever, but never gimmicky. You are given a tin of granola and a printout of your menu upon departure, but a meal like this is not soon to be forgotten, even without goody bags.

THE UNION SQUARE CRAWL

1. **BREADS BAKERY,** 18 E. 16TH ST., NEW YORK, (212) 633-2253, BREADSBAKERY.COM

2. **TSURUTONTAN,** 21 E. 16TH ST., NEW YORK, (212) 989-1000, TSURUTONTAN.COM

3. **PETE'S TAVERN,** 129 E. 18TH ST., NEW YORK, (212) 473-7676, PETESTAVERN.COM

4. **CASA MONO,** 52 IRVING PLACE, NEW YORK, (212) 253-2773, CASAMONONYC.COM

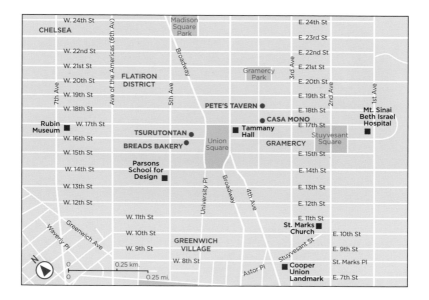

Union Square

It's Hip to Be Square

UNION SQUARE HAS LONG REPRESENTED THE BEGINNING OF "DOWNTOWN," separating the factions claiming never to go above or below 14th Street. Union Square Park acts as the nucleus of the area, with Greenwich Village extending below it, the East Village to the right and West Village to the left. The park itself attracts a varied mix of characters, from protesters, chanting Hare Krishnas, street artists, and skateboarders, to people just trying to get to the subway, college students, etc. The Union Square Greenmarket is open Monday, Wednesday, Friday, and Saturday year-round, and sees up to 60,000 people daily passing through to peruse the bounty of fresh produce, meats, baked goods, and cheeses. If you are there early enough, you might even spot some top chefs poking around and gathering goods that inspire them.

Union Square has gone through many shifts of identity over the years, and now presents a more homogenized version of itself, flanked with big-box retailers and luxury condos. The restaurant scene is a mix of old-time haunts and ambitious up-and-comers. Fun fact: The south side of 14th Street features a large condo with an electronic display of constantly changing numbers whose meaning has been guessed to be everything from the national debt to the number of lives lost to smoking. Impress your friend with your knowledge—the numbers display the time.

1 BREADS BAKERY

In just over four years, **BREADS BAKERY** has established itself as an indispensable part of the sweets scene, thanks in large part to its now famous chocolate babka, but the savory items and handmade breads are just as worthy of praise and extra gym time. Everything at Breads is of the highest quality, and the offerings are a little more unexpected than at your average bakery; think flaky croissants and righteous rugelach, chewy cheese straws, stuffed spinach pies, glorious homemade challahs, that famous babka . . . and that is just the front room. If you can resist the tempting smells and make your way to the back portion, you will be rewarded with the premade sandwiches and salads as well as coffee, tea, etc. Everything is made on the

premises throughout the day to ensure maximum freshness, and you can feel the love in each item. The secret to the babka is Nutella, and if you really want to get your hands dirty, Breads offers classes, so you can roll your own.

2 TSURUTONTAN

Ramen gets a lot of attention, but udon is so much more than just its chubby sibling, and **TSURUTONTAN** is the ideal spot to get your udon on. Located in the original Union Square Café space, TsuruTonTan is a rather upscale slurping establishment, with many seating areas and options, from communal bars to proper tables. As large as it is, there are often waits, so take advantage of the fact that they offer reservations. TsuruTonTan has twelve locations in Japan, and its founder opened their first handmade udon restaurant in 1979. They take immense pride in their noodles and pay great attention to the entire experience, down to the bowls the udon is served in. The menu is large and has photos to help with the dish descriptions; some of the dishes are cold, some are not served in broth, and there are rice bowls as well. The noodles themselves are addicting, and slurping and chewing them is downright fun.

"Tsuru"—the sound of slurping noodles

"Ton"—the sound of kneading and shaping noodles

"Tan"—the sound of cutting noodles

3 PETE'S TAVERN

PETE'S TAVERN has been wetting the whistles of thirsty New Yorkers since 1864, and takes great pride in being the tavern where O'Henry drank. Pete's has charm galore, aided by its location on Irving Place, a tiny street with beautiful historic appeal, bordered by Union Square and Gramercy Park. Pete's has a classic speakeasy feel with brick walls and checkerboard floors, and the rambling collection of back rooms and upstairs hideaways enhances the Prohibition vibe. The front bar area is the most action-packed, especially during the holiday season, when the ceiling is draped in an endless sea of lights. During warmer months outdoor seating is the perfect place to hunker down and enjoy a few rounds and watch the world go by. Pete's food is a mix of typical bar bites mixed with Italian specialties, and it is best to keep it simple and make drinks the top priority; after enough of those you may write like O'Henry as well.

4

CASA MONO

Spain's Costa Brava serves some of the most adventurous and ambitious food in the world, a mix of unusual proteins and fresh flavors that is unique to the region—and to **CASA MONO**. Casa Mono is truly transporting, a trip to the coast just blocks from Union Square, a tiny spot always bursting with energy emanating from the open kitchen. Sitting at the counter is a show, as all of the dishes are composed right in front of your eyes. The walls are lined with bottles of sherry and table wine, and the mostly Spanish wine list offers a chance to expand your vino horizons. The dish to get is the fideos with chorizo, sea bream, and clams, with the toasty noodles soaking up all the salty, briny flavor yet still maintaining their texture. All of the dishes are true tapas style, and even the bigger plates are not overwhelming, so you can feel free to go a bit overboard, and definitely share. Bar Jamon next door is the perfect spot for some drinks and ham while you wait for a table, or is a cozy destination in its own right.

THE GREENWICH VILLAGE CRAWL

1. **BAR PITTI,** 268 6TH AVE., NEW YORK, (212) 982-3300

2. **MINETTA TAVERN,** 113 MACDOUGAL ST., NEW YORK, (212) 475-3850, MINETTATAVERNNY.COM

3. **MAMOUN'S,** 119 MACDOUGAL ST., NEW YORK, MAMOUNS.COM

4. **GOTHAM BAR AND GRILL,** 12 E. 12TH ST., NEW YORK, (212) 620-4020, GOTHAMBARANDGRILL.COM

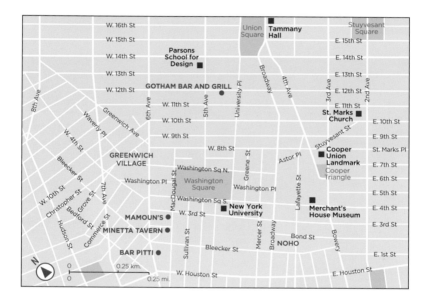

Greenwich Village

The Place to See What's UP DOWNtown

GREENWICH VILLAGE, OR "THE VILLAGE" WAS THE EPICENTER OF 1960S COUNTERCULTURE, a bohemian artists' enclave that welcomed free-thinkers and sprouted many progressive ideas and movements. Greenwich Village has a rich legacy of embracing the arts and having a forward-thinking, inclusive nature; it was home to the first racially integrated nightclub and has been a long-standing hub for the LGBT community. The folk music scene of the 1960s was based in the Village, and it still has many highly regarded jazz clubs. Washington Square Park with its glorious arch is a scenic, bustling microcosm of life in the Village. It attracts students, performers, fancy dogs, and possibly a rogue pot dealer and acts as the core of the area. Restaurants in the area are a mix of evergreen fashionable spots, old-school charmers, student-friendly cheap bites, and established elegant eateries.

1 BAR PITTI

BAR PITTI is the watering hole of choice for the true jet-set fashion crowd, the glamorous group that follows the roving party from continent to continent looking fabulous and inciting envy in every wannabe "influencer" with an iPhone and a dream. In the warm months, sitting outside at Pitti allows a front-row seat to air kissing and greetings shouted in Italian, and during the winter months the small space is packed with fur coats casually thrown over chairs. Bar Pitti is an authentic Italian taverna, with a lengthy board of specials and a dolce vita attitude, except when it comes to reservations (no) and credit cards (no). The food is prepared in proper Italian fashion, utilizing seasonal, high-quality ingredients and treated simply. Their namesake dish, the Rigatoni Pitti, is not to be missed, and the meatballs are worth fighting for, as the original owners did. Pitti will have you feeling well fed and fabulous, especially at the prices, which are reasonable no matter the exchange rate.

2 MINETTA TAVERN

The original **MINETTA TAVERN** opened in 1937, and attracted various literary personalities such as Ernest Hemingway, E. E. Cummings, and Eugene O'Neill. It is unclear if they would have made the cut after the restaurant got a fancy refresh in 2009, courtesy of King of Buzz Keith McNally. Proving that everything that is old is new again, Minetta Tavern has settled into its groove as a celebrity-friendly, meat-centric bistro that is so charming you want to pinch it on the cheeks. The restaurant features just 70 seats over two rooms, and the front bar area gets quite busy as it doubles as holding pen for those waiting for tables as well as those waiting for drinks or a seat at the bar. The Black Label Burger, a $26 burger made from a custom blend of dry aged meat, is often the biggest celebrity in the room, but not necessarily the most talented. The Minetta Burger is just as good and comes with fries, and many of the meat dishes are extraordinary. The bistro options are all solid, and solidly filling, and brunch also features finely executed French fare, without some of the crowds. Minetta Tavern would seem like a restaurant you would encounter in Paris, but is very historically New York.

3

MAMOUN'S

MAMOUN'S is perfectly located to feed a never-ending supply of drunk, hungry people looking to eat on a budget. Its proximity to NYU, the bars and clubs on MacDougal, and its long operating hours help to explain its popularity since 1971; the flavors and quality should also be given proper credit. Mamoun's is

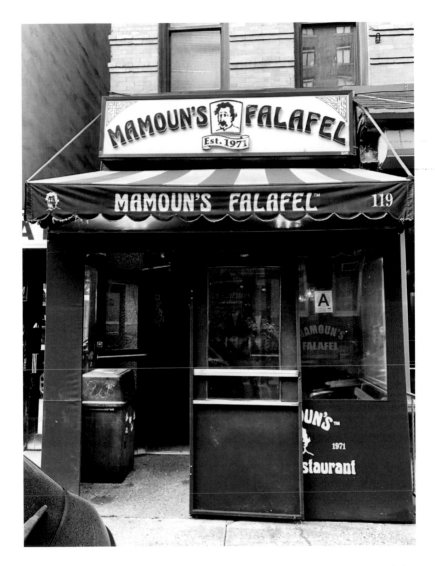

regarded as the first falafel restaurant in New York City and one of the first Middle Eastern restaurants in the United States, which is worth noting, especially as it seems almost every food cart in the city serves some variation of Middle Eastern fare. The restaurant is small, family owned and operated, and taking your food to go is the best option. Find a bench in nearby Washington Square Park or walk and eat, which runs the risk of tahini dripping down your sleeve. The food is authentic and straightforward, bursting with flavor; the pitas are also bursting, stuffed however you choose, but the falafel and shawarma are both outstanding.

4 GOTHAM BAR AND GRILL

GOTHAM BAR AND GRILL is an adult restaurant, sophisticated and elegant, a sparkling oasis of sport jackets in traditionally casual downtown. Since 1984 Gotham has been serving refined American cuisine, and is regularly recognized as one of the best restaurants in the city. The vibe is upscale yet approachable, and there is a large bar that is ideal for a slightly more casual dining experience. During the day the dining room is flooded with light, and at night the room has a soft glow, setting the scene for clinking glasses and sparkling conversation. Unlike other chefs who tend to expand their focus when their name is established, Chef Alfred Portale remains a part of Gotham Bar and Grill, and still sources the Greenmarket for each day's specials. Gotham Bar and Grill feels both fresh and classic and is still very much a relevant part of the New York dining scene, especially downtown.

THE EAST VILLAGE CRAWL

1. **CAFÉ MOGADOR,** 101 ST. MARKS PLACE #1, NEW YORK, (212) 677-2226, CAFEMOGADOR.COM

2. **MOMOFUKU NOODLE BAR,** 171 1ST AVE., NEW YORK, (212) 777-7773, NOODLEBAR-NY.MOMOFUKU.COM

3. **XI'AN FAMOUS FOODS,** 81 ST. MARKS PLACE, NEW YORK, XIANFOODS.COM

4. **SUPPER,** 156 E. 2ND ST., NEW YORK, (212) 477-7600, SUPPERRESTAURANT.COM

5. **ANGEL'S SHARE,** 8 STUYVESANT ST., NEW YORK, (212) 777-5415

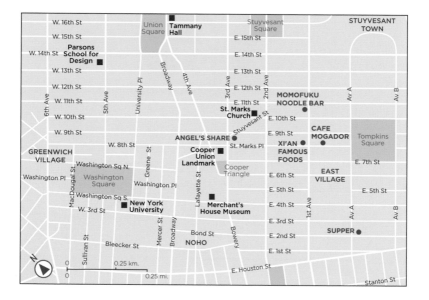

East Village

Around the World without a Passport

THE PUNKS ARE GONE FROM CBGB'S, and there is a Chipotle on St. Mark's, but the East Village still has a little edge to it. The rolling tides of gentrification mean that the East Village is currently more new development than dirty needle, and while shiny new luxury condos might indicate otherwise, the East Village is one of the last bastions of affordable commercial space for restaurants in Manhattan. This affordability and the neighborhood's proximity to NYU ensure that there are still high-quality cheap eats available at many hours of the day. Whereas other neighborhoods may be firmly associated with only certain types of cuisine, the East Village is home to every sort of flavor, from Middle Eastern to Korean and everything in between.

1

CAFÉ MOGADOR

Jumpstart your day with a Turkish coffee and some breakfast from **CAFÉ MOGADOR,** and pat yourself on the back for knowing about this gem of a restaurant. Although crawling with those who consider brunch a sport on the weekends, weekdays also offer breakfast until 4 pm, in addition to their full lunch and dinner menus. The atmosphere is subtly evocative of the Middle East, with bright white walls and dark accents, somehow both cozy in the winter and light and airy in the summer. It is hard to find such quality Middle Eastern food in such a pleasant atmosphere anywhere in the city, a testament to how this spot has survived for almost 35 years. The Middle Eastern breakfast is beautiful in its simplicity, each element executed perfectly: eggs cooked to your liking, creamy hummus with a pool of olive oil, tabbouleh bright with acid, a well-dressed salad, and of course clouds of za'atar-dusted pita. The falafel is also head and shoulders above what you would get from a street cart, and not much more expensive.

2 MOMOFUKU NOODLE BAR

Yes, this is name-brand ramen, but David Chang is as famous as is he is for good reason, and **MOMOFUKU NOODLE BAR** is the best place to experience the swagger and flavors that started a movement. There are often long lines and foodie tourists,

so the best bet is to go alone and snag a seat at one of the counters for an early lunch or dinner, or pop in late at night. Sitting in front of the open kitchen is better than watching a cooking class, and hearing the expediter call the orders never gets old. The space is all blond wood and a little cramped, but you will make quick friends with your neighbor as you slurp on your noodles and share the ssam sauce. The food has a Korean tilt, which is often reflected in the specials, and of course there's excellent kimchi. The pork buns are gloriously melty, the sweetness of the sauce and the bun balanced by the snap of a cucumber. The Momofuku ramen has a broth unlike any other, full of umami, and the noodles are thin and curly and fun to eat. If you have a group, and are able to plan ahead, Noodle Bar offers large-format fried chicken lunches and dinners that are truly special. And to really celebrate, Chang offers a fried chicken and caviar meal, which is the true embodiment of high/low cuisine at its finest. It's clucking phenomenal. . . .

XI'AN FAMOUS FOODS

Rare is the restaurant that begins with an "X," but that is just the beginning of what is special about **XI'AN FAMOUS FOODS**. There are several locations of this family-run mini-chain that started in a basement food court in Flushing, each outpost an homage to their home region in China. The decor is relatively bare bones, the few seats are along the walls, below pictures of the menu items and framed press pieces, and there is no bathroom. Most notable are two important signs in the restaurant, one regarding the integrity of their proprietary hot oil, and another that says the following:

"WARNING: PLEASE READ: Food tastes best when fresh from the kitchen. When hot noodles cool down, they get bloated, mushy, and oily. If you must take your noodles to go, please at least try the noodles in the store or right out of the to-go container when it's handed to you, so you can get the best possible Xi'an Famous Foods experience." Their signature dish that brings the long lines is the N1, spicy lamb cumin noodles. Once you taste this dish, you will understand why the noodles are described as "hand-ripped," and just how special that makes them; the texture is firm and springy, toothsome, totally unlike any other noodle. The lamb is seasoned with a kick of spice, making the dish addicting in its depth of flavor and texture. Other notable dishes include the spicy cumin lamb burger, and the spicy oxtail soup with hand-ripped noodles. Even after the ramen at Momofuku, there should always be room for a quick trip to Xi'an.

4

SUPPER

Supper and its sister restaurants Frank and Lil' Frankie's are part of the neighborhood fabric of the East Village, solid Italian spots that feel genuine and a little quirky. All the restaurants bear signs of being related while maintaining their own identities, the most common thread being the nostalgia-inducing Italian comfort food and their aversion to credit cards (thankfully most of them now take reservations). Supper is romantic but fun, candlelit with brick walls and an open kitchen, and offers only beer and wine. Extensive daily specials supplement the already tempting menu, including the Spaghetti Limone, a marvel of creamy Parmesan and bright hints of lemon served in a heaping portion that all too quickly seems to disappear. Supper also has a fantastic, intimate private room that does not require a minimum to reserve, perfect for any last-minute celebrations.

ANGEL'S SHARE

ANGEL'S SHARE is a very special place, a Tokyo-style speakeasy hidden atop an unassuming izakaya restaurant across from an NYU dorm. Although now easily found by its lines of waiting people, Angel's Share is accessed by entering Village Yokocho, walking up the stairs, turning left, and opening the unmarked door. Angel's Share is small, and the vibe is quiet and respectful, encouraging everyone to be properly reverent toward the cocktail

craftsmanship practiced here. The best way to experience this spot and its decorum is to arrive early and with a small group. In the dim lights and under a mural depicting the namesake angels, the vest-clad bartenders take meticulous care to create Japanese-accented takes on classic cocktails; don't be surprised to see ingredients being smoked or exposed to liquid nitrogen. Angel Share will impress any date, but can also be properly experienced alone.

If secret bars are your thing, there is another in the East Village that is worth seeking out, literally: *Please Don't Tell*, or *PDT*. Accessed through a phone booth in hot dog heaven Crif Dogs, *PDT* serves hand-crafted cocktails alongside any of Crif Dog's munchies friendly fare, including their bacon-wrapped hot dogs. Contrary to the secrecy applied in the name, plenty of people have told their friends about *PDT*, so it is best to reserve if possible, when the phone lines open each afternoon.

113 St. Marks Pl., New York (212) 614-0386; Pdtnyc.com

THE WEST VILLAGE CRAWL

1. **MARY'S FISH CAMP,** 64 CHARLES ST., NEW YORK, (646) 486-2185, MARYSFISHCAMP.COM

2. **BAR SARDINE,** 183 W. 10TH ST., NEW YORK, (646) 360-3705, BARSARDINENYC.COM

3. **L'ARTUSI,** 228 W. 10TH ST., NEW YORK, (212) 255-5757, LARTUSI.COM

4. **BIG GAY ICE CREAM,** 61 GROVE ST., NEW YORK, BIGGAYICECREAM.COM

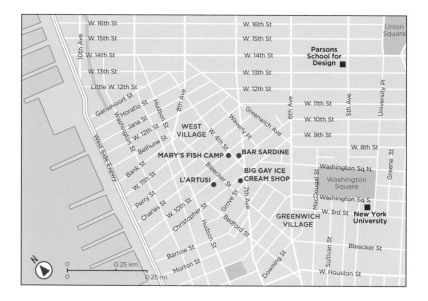

The West Village

Eat like a Local

THE WEST VILLAGE IS THE ROM-COM MOVIE SET OF NEW YORK CITY, a picturesque and charming neighborhood that is ideal for strolling hand in hand, marveling at the endless display of real estate porn. The West Village has an abundance of classic character, found in its tree-lined and brownstone-filled cobblestone streets, which are now sprinkled with modern, edgy architectural marvels and prime shopping, all combining to make this an easy neighborhood in which to while away a day. The food options include everything from big-name chefs like Jean Georges Vongerichten and Dominique Ansel to ambitious up-and-comers. In warmer months there is nothing better than a stroll along the many parks on the Hudson River followed by drinks and bites outside while actively but slyly people-watching; many "low-key" celebrities call the neighborhood home. In the winter the snow on the trees blankets the neighborhood with a poetic hush, which is more magical than even a Hollywood set. Many restaurants do not accept reservations, and the ones that do often offer seats at the bar on a first-come basis, to allow for locals. Looking like a local means refraining from taking pictures in front of Magnolia Bakery, carrying a $10 coffee, and affecting just the right amount of downtown indifference.

1 MARY'S FISH CAMP

Nothing bring the "claws" out of passionate foodies like a debate over the best lobster roll in New York City. The version at **MARY'S FISH CAMP** is always mentioned as one of city's top, and for good reason. Mary's lobster roll is a thing of beauty—a perfectly warmed, toasted, and buttered split hot dog bun overflowing with huge pink chunks of mayo'd lobster, and accompanied by a heaping pile of crunchy, skinny fries, just begging to be doused in the always handy vinegar. Although the lobster roll is their most famous item, there's no shortage of crave-worthy catches on the menu, including the oyster po'boy, the shrimp burger, the daily fish, oysters, etc. If there is room for dessert, there is a decadent ice cream sundae and often homemade cobblers. Mary's is tiny, its decor evoking a small seaside restaurant that you feel lucky to have stumbled upon, and if you are able to snag a seat, then lucky you are.

2 BAR SARDINE

BAR SARDINE is also movie-ready, the ideal setting for a perfect first date for the couple who had a meet-cute in the quirky salt store down the street. A thin wisp of a place, the many candles throw a glow that make everyone look like an Instagram filter, and close quarters makes it easy to find an excuse to snuggle up to your neighbor. Bar Sardine takes its cocktails and its food very seriously, and each offering shows subtle but substantial skill and pride, without any pretense. This is an ideal spot to come early for a drink and stay late into the night, ordering bites as the whim hits. Warm weather means open windows, but the real draw all year is the burger, a gorgeously messy combination of meat, smoked cheddar, crisp cucumbers, and their special BBQ sauce, something to fall in love with even if the date doesn't work out.

3 L'ARTUSI

There is a lot to love about **L'ARTUSI**, a restaurant that serves destination-worthy food but maintains its neighborhood charm. L'Artusi is as hard to get into as it was when it first opened, which is no small accomplishment in New York City. The atmosphere is quintessential West Village—a mix of a cool, buzzy hot spot and a neighborhood joint that is completely organic and not contrived. The real action is downstairs, which features a large bar where you can dine and watch the kitchen, as well as cozy tables and banquettes. Upstairs is removed from the activity in the kitchen, but is pleasant nonetheless, not at all Siberia-like. L'Artusi offers high-quality Italian ingredients done in simple interpretations to maximize their flavors. There are no "typical" Italian dishes, but the combinations are both familiar and inventive.

The absolute best dish at L'Artusi is the roasted mushrooms with pancetta, chilies, and ricotta *salata*. This dish is an ingenious example of how seemingly simple preparation and ingredients can create something magical. The pastas are all cooked perfectly, and we have tried almost all of them. Our favorites are the spaghetti with garlic, Parmesan and chilies; the *bucatini* with tomato, pancetta, and pecorino (similar to an Amatriciana, really clean and spicy); the tagliatelle with Bolognese *bianco* (definitely the best interpretation of this dish that we have ever tried); and of course the famous *orecchiette* with sausage, salami, and radicchio. On the less carby side, there are fresh crudos and well-constructed proteins, including a hanger steak with crispy potatoes and a salsa *bianco* that could make a meat-eater out of anyone. L'Artusi is a true neighborhood place, if your neighborhood happens to be the coolest in New York City.

4 BIG GAY ICE CREAM

A rainbow-flecked temple to unicorns and whimsy, **BIG GAY ICE CREAM** is the brick-and-mortar outpost of what originally started as an ice cream truck, an adult Willy Wonka's palace with a bit of a naughty streak. Located across from the famous Stonewall Inn and Christopher Street, Big Gay Ice Cream pays homage to the historically gay-friendly neighborhood with a flair that it is all its own. In case the name is not a giveaway, this is a place that does not take itself too seriously, except when it comes to quality and flavor, two common elements of every item on their menu. After dinner or a drink in the neighborhood, head in for a Salty Pimp, and prepare to have your life changed: vanilla softserve covered in a layer of dulce de leche, then coated with a hard casing of salty dark chocolate, on a cone no less. They also make pints to bring home, as well as a cookbook. The shop is small and often attracts lines of customers ready to post their colorful creations to Instagram, especially in the warmer months, so be prepared to wait.

THE BLEECKER STREET CRAWL

1. **JOHN'S OF BLEECKER,** 278 BLEECKER ST., NEW YORK, (212) 243-1680, JOHNSBRICKOVENPIZZA.COM

2. **FAICCO'S ITALIAN SPECIALTIES,** 260 BLEECKER ST., NEW YORK, (212) 243-1974

3. **MURRAY'S CHEESE SHOP,** 254 BLEECKER ST., NEW YORK, (212) 243-3289, MURRAYSCHEESE.COM

4. **JOE'S,** 7 CARMINE ST., NEW YORK, (212) 366-1182, JOESPIZZANYC.COM

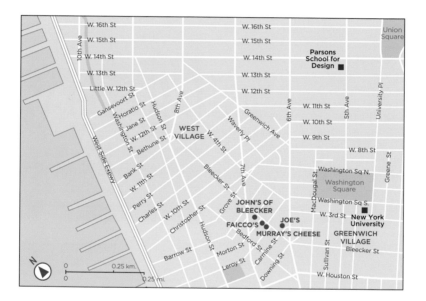

Bleecker Street

Eat the Street

BLEECKER STREET RUNS FROM EIGHTH AVENUE ALL THE WAY ACROSS TO THE BOWERY, one of the few east-west streets in New York City to span both the West and East Villages. Along its rambling crosstown route, Bleecker Street has many personalities; it is home to many luxury brands in the West Village, and comedy clubs and NYU hangouts a bit farther east. Also of note, but not included in this crawl or the West Village crawl is Magnolia Bakery on the corner of Bleecker Street and West 11th Street; if sweets are important, the banana bread pudding surpasses the cupcakes, but don't wait in line for more than 10 minutes.

The stretch of Bleecker Street covered in this crawl is between 7th and 6th Avenues, home primarily to multigeneration Italian businesses. Although Murray's Cheese has expanded and is available for mail order, and Joe's Pizza now has several locations throughout the city, the experience offered at all of these spots is authentic and their commitment to quality is apparent. The commerce on Bleecker Street is largely free of big box retailers (there is a L'Occitane, but nowadays nothing is completely immune to chains), and instead offers old-world charm.

1

JOHN'S OF BLEECKER

No slices! **JOHN'S** serves a slice of history, if not the best pizza in town, and it is where a crawl east on Bleecker Street should start. John's is one of the longest running establishments on Bleecker Street, and its straightforward devotion to its pizza is charming. The room is wood paneled and its heritage obvious—the wooden benches and walls have years' worth of carvings, marks that have stood the test of time longer than the romances they originally signified, and the black-and-white checkerboard floor is well worn.

Opened in 1929, John's is still family-run, and they make their pizza in a coal-fired brick oven. The finished product is a thick-ish dough that is sturdy enough to stand up to the cheese and sauce, but soft enough to have some chew. The crust is crunchy, with some good char from the coal. John's is a piece of history in the form of a piece of pizza, and needs to be experienced.

2 FAICCO'S ITALIAN SPECIALTIES

FAICCO'S is the sort of Italian deli anyone would be lucky to have in their neighborhood, chock full of all of the Italian deli staples to keep your belly and pantry full: homemade "mozz" and prepared stuffed breads, chicken cutlets, roasted peppers, pastas of every shape, homemade sausages, and of course frozen pizza dough. In addition to all the meats, cheeses, and oils, the shelves are packed with imported Italian specialties, and everything is fresh and the real deal, even if most of the shoppers no longer live in the neighborhood. The real draw at Faicco's is their sandwiches, created with love from all of their quality ingredients; the chicken, pesto, and mozzarella is heavy enough to put your luggage over the weight limit, but worth smuggling home. The Italian hero is one of the best in the city,

piled high with all the pork cold cuts, proving the trite adage that not all heroes wear capes. Faicco's has been around since 1900, with the fourth generation now in charge, and the authenticity is palpable; if you want your sandwich on gluten-free whole-grain, fuggetaboutit!

3 MURRAY'S CHEESE SHOP

Not to be cheesy, but **MURRAY'S** is whey fabulous! Murray's is a one-stop shop for all things cheese and cheese adjacent; they carry endless varieties of crackers, nuts familiar and exotic, brined vegetables, salty dried meats, breads, etc. Everything you need to create the ultimate entertaining platter is available, including hard-to-find European canned goods (sardines, Italian tuna), and cheese knives. However if the selection of cheeses seems overwhelming, there are premade platters and grab-and-go items, and the staff is friendly and happy to help, as well as dole out samples. Murray's has their own cheese caves, as well as rooms for their on-site classes. Murray's offers made to order sandwiches, including the best grilled cheese in New York City (served on Orwasher's bread) and decadent breakfast sandwiches. There is a small seating area to dig in while it's hot (you won't be able to resist), and in nicer weather you can sit on a bench outside or take it to the small park near 6th Avenue. If you are a die-hard dairy fan and simply cannot get enough cheese, Murray's also has a sit-down restaurant serving (one guess) all things cheese, including righteous mac 'n' cheese options and fondue, as well as some wine, which officially makes cheese a meal when served together.

4

JOE'S

Until recently it was considered a political scandal if a politician ate New York pizza with a knife and fork; times have changed, but eating Joe's with cutlery could still be considered a punishable offense. **JOE'S** is the ultimate New York City slice; a piping-hot triangle of pizza, intended to be eaten immediately, standing up, folded in half and dripping with cheese and oil. A slice of Joe's is now $3, but it is worth it; the sauce is sweet and fresh, and the cheese is high quality and in the right proportion. The store itself is now on Carmine, relocated from the original Bleecker Street location around the corner. It is tiny, the photos and newspaper clippings on its walls a testament to its enduring popularity and celebrity following. Grab your slice (or pie) and get out of the way, and get it into your face as soon as possible. Joe's is a bite of New York City, any time of day or night.

TIP

To fully exhaust the pizza options on Bleecker Street, you can also check out Bleecker Street Pizza (69 7th Avenue South); their plain slices as well as their thicker-crust Grandma slices are quite exceptional.

THE CHELSEA / MEATPACKING CRAWL

1. **BARBUTO,** 775 WASHINGTON ST., NEW YORK, (212) 924-9700, BARBUTONYC.COM

2. **EL QUINTO PINO,** 401 W. 24TH ST., NEW YORK, (212) 206-6900, ELQUINTOPINONYC.COM

3. **THE RED CAT,** 227 10TH AVE., NEW YORK, (212) 242-1308, THEREDCAT.COM

4. **THE TOP OF THE STANDARD,** THE STANDARD HIGH LINE, NEW YORK, 848 WASHINGTON ST., (212) 645-7600, STANDARDHOTELS.COM/NEW-YORK/FEATURES/TOP-OF-THE-STANDARD

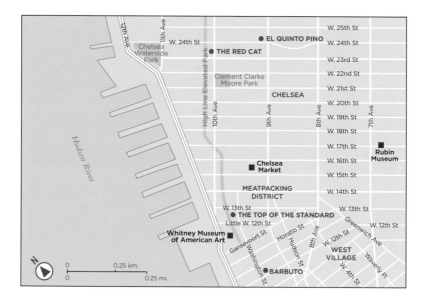

Chelsea / Meatpacking

Eating the High Line

THE HIGH LINE IS A RAMBLING, WINDING PUBLIC PARK built on an old railroad track extending from Gansevoort to 34th Street, between 10th and 12th Avenues. It's a special way to experience the West Side of Manhattan, with extraordinary views and surprising design elements around every corner; all of the flora and fauna are varieties that were naturally growing over the abandoned tracks. Walking the High Line from beginning to end will allow you to explore the Meatpacking District and Chelsea. While the northern limit of the High Line may currently seem a bit desolate, the upcoming opening of Hudson Yards is set to breathe new life into the area and make it a destination in its own right. For art lovers, the High Line provides a perfect way to spend an afternoon, beginning at the Whitney Museum and ending among the galleries in Chelsea. All of this culture and walking will of course require proper nourishment, and there is no shortage of spots to keep you well fed and ready to explore. There is no judgment if art perusing becomes shopping at Jeffrey—some of their items are works of art in their own right.

1 BARBUTO

Slightly south of the Whitney, **BARBUTO** is the perfect spot to carbo-load for the rest of the day. When the weather allows the huge garage doors are flung open, allowing the fresh air and the buzz of the area to infiltrate every pore of the already happening restaurant. Jonathan Waxman is the king of California cuisine; his Italian-style fare at Barbuto is fresh and comforting, and you can taste his personality and

skill in every bite. The JW Chicken with salsa verde is bright and juicy, and the brunch/lunch-only *bucatini carbonara* is a crowd pleaser. On the lighter side the kale Caesar salad is about as good as kale can taste. Barbuto is casual and very much of the neighborhood, a place that will make you want to plan your return as soon as you leave.

2 EL QUINTO PINO

EL QUINTO PINO is small in size but makes a big impression. This tapas bar was so popular that they eventually added an additional dining room to accommodate demand, and it is not hard to see why. Uniquely imagined takes on traditional tapas are served alongside unexpected wine selections in a laid-back, authentic environment; basically, it is a really cool spot. Tapas staples like *pan amb tomaca* (tomato bread), garlic shrimp, and *patatas bravas* are available as well as more exotic options like an *uni panini*. Everything is well executed, and it is easy to be drawn in by the charms of El Quinto Pino; no one will blame you if you decide to blow off the rest of your plans and sit and order food and drinks indefinitely.

3

THE RED CAT

Jimmy Bradley's **THE RED CAT** is the go-to spot for gallerinas and their friends. Casual and elegant, it sets itself apart with its straightforward commitment to outstanding food and unpretentious service. The Red Cat serves many purposes for the neighborhood, from business lunch to lively drinks, and is even a perfect spot to sit at the bar solo and dine before or after a day at the galleries. The vegetable dishes are especially outstanding, and the tempura-fried green beans can convert a carnivore. The people-watching is also quite delicious.

4

THE TOP OF THE STANDARD

THE TOP OF THE STANDARD has top-notch views, and top-notch snob appeal to match. You have to know someone or be someone to get in here after dark, all for the privilege of sipping $25 martinis with an almost 360-degree view. Fret not mere mortals, there is hope: As long as there is not a private event, the bar is open from 4 to 9 pm with no pretense, provided you are not dressed like you were pulled out of the Hudson River. Although the Beautiful People may own the night, sunset is a magical time to experience the bar. The room is breathtaking in its own right, with flattering lighting and a show-stopping bar, everything giving off a Deco vibe and oozing of fabulousness. It is worth stopping in for the view from the bathrooms alone—there is really no experience quite like it.

THE SOHO CRAWL

1. **BALTHAZAR,** 80 SPRING ST., NEW YORK,(212) 965-1414, BALTHAZARNY.COM

2. **LE COUCOU,** 138 LAFAYETTE ST., NEW YORK, (212) 271-4252, LECOUCOU.COM

3. **RAOUL'S,** 180 PRINCE ST., NEW YORK, (212) 966-3518

4. **LURE,** 142 MERCER ST., NEW YORK, (212) 431-7676, LUREFISHBAR.COM

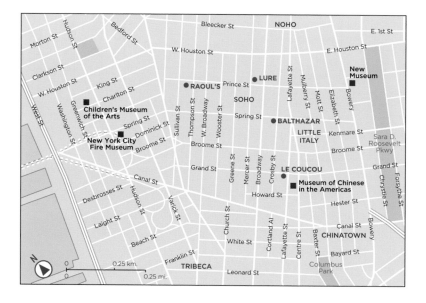

SoHo

Swanky Swagger

BEFORE THE BIGGEST NAMES IN RETAIL LINED ITS COBBLE-STONED STREETS, SoHo was full of the soon to be biggest names in art. SoHo boasts the largest amount of cast-iron architecture in the world. Before the lofts therein commanded big money, they were hives of creativity, with artists like Keith Haring and Jean-Michel Basquiat taking advantage of the large spaces with natural light to live and create.

SoHo's art legacy can still be seen in the galleries scattered around, but the avant-garde vibe is all but gone, replaced with retail therapy. SoHo is home to some of the biggest names in international luxury, with the shopping here rivaled only by Madison Avenue. Shopping and playing in SoHo is chic chic chic, but never cheap cheap cheap. To look like you belong, adopt a look of pained inconvenience as you brush past the crowds, and know that a bag full of leftovers is always the bag of the season.

1

BALTHAZAR

After twenty years, **BALTHAZAR** still packs a chic Parisian punch. There is something magic about the experience at Balthazar that is somehow greater than all of its parts, which are all pretty special. Now more tourist-friendly than the impossible reservation it once was, Balthazar still attracts all the pretty people who could actually be in a brasserie in Paris rather than a French brasserie in New York City. Every meal at Balthazar is a treat, and they serve all three. Breakfast takes advantage of the made-in-house pastries from the bakery next door, and lunch and dinner have finely executed bistro classics. The french fries are perfection, on their own or paired with the steak, but especially with a nice glass of wine. If pounding the pavement in the shops of SoHo has your feet aching for a break, there is no better place to regroup than the bar at Balthazar.

2

LE COUCOU

LE COUCOU is le stunning from the moment you walk in. The bar area is small, well articulated, meticulous in its design but never being too precious. The Roman and Williams–designed dining room is beautiful, basically divided into front and back areas, anchored by a large wall of windows in the front and the pristine, bustling open kitchen in the back. Chef Daniel Rose is an American who made a big splash in Paris, and Le CouCou marks his return to the US. His talents are on full display (literally) as the open kitchen churns and fires on all cylinders. Breakfast at Le CouCou feels like eating in your hotel on the Left Bank, lunch is flooded with light from the large windows, and dinner feels special but not too buttoned up, a very modern way of fine dining for every meal. The menu is unexpected and reaps big rewards when risks are taken, and service is polished and helpful. To experience Le CouCou is to experience upscale downtown dining at its finest.

3 RAOUL'S

RAOUL'S is an old-school SoHo institution, long regarded as a top date spot in New York City. It is dark and a bit cramped and full of character, including a palm reader available outside the bathrooms. Raoul's will keep all of your secrets, and is always up for another drink, but in order to taste the best of Raoul's, you will need to be there during daylight. The reason: Raoul's only offers their burger during brunch or in limited quantities (12) at the bar each night. In a city of special burgers, Raoul's is worth seeking out; departed and beloved burger expert Josh Ozersky once called it "the best burger in America." The meat is Pat LaFrieda, and the special sauce, quite literally, is au poivre, in several forms, with the whole creation cradled between two pieces of challah roll. Take a moment to take in the art on the walls of Raoul's—you might get more than an eyeful.

4 LURE FISHBAR

The allure of **LURE FISHBAR** is easy to figure out: Luxury motor yacht decor, crowd-pleasing menu, and consistently good food make it a no-brainer for brunch, lunch, or dinner. It doesn't get much more fashionable than a location underneath the Prada store and across from the Mercer Hotel, which makes Lure the optimal spot for a SoHo canteen. (Fun fact: The previous occupant of the Lure space was a beloved restaurant called Canteen.) Chef Josh Capon proves himself to be a jack of all trades, equally adept at bar bites like chicken lollipops, subtly sauced seafood dishes, and gut-busting burgers, as well as the raw bar, sushi, and brunch items that are served.

Lure is equally appropriate for any occasion that draws you to SoHo, whether it be the festive dinner before a big night out, the hair of the dog brunch the next morning, or even a big family lunch. It is impossible not to find something that suits you on the Lure menu, which can also be said about the Prada store above. Lure is enduringly popular and often busy, but its size makes a reservation easy to snag, unlike that last pair of Prada shoes on sale.

THE CHINATOWN CRAWL

1. **LAM ZHOU HANDMADE NOODLE,** 40 BOWERY, NEW YORK, (212) 566-6933

2. **GREAT NEW YORK NOODLETOWN,** 28 BOWERY, NEW YORK, (212) 349-0923, GREATNYNOODLETOWN.COM

3. **NOM WAH TEA PARLOR,** 13 DOYERS ST., NEW YORK, (212) 962-6047, NOMWAH.COM

4. **JING FONG,** 20 ELIZABETH ST., NEW YORK, (212) 964-5256, JINGFONGY.COM

5. **10BELOW,** 10 MOTT ST., NEW YORK, 10BELOWICECREAM.COM

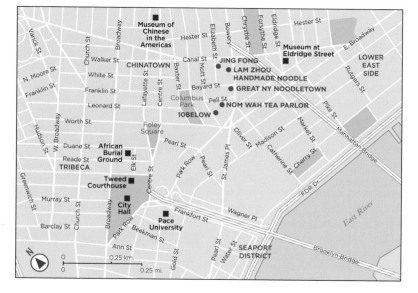

Chinatown

Dim Sum and then Some

NEW YORK CITY'S CHINATOWN IS AN EXCITING EXPERIENCE FOR ALL SENSES, a crowded, bustling enclave whose residents faithfully adhere to traditions brought over from the Far East. New York City's Chinatown boasts the largest Chinese population of any city outside of Asia, and a visit to the area is truly transporting. Beyond cuisines of China (Cantonese, Szechuan, Shanghainese, and more), the food options available span many countries including Thailand, Singapore, Indonesia, and Japan. Restaurants range from tiny storefronts to huge establishments that take up entire blocks, and there are markets catering to every type of exotic delicacy, including the noxiously fragrant durian and live eels. The only inauthentic element about Chinatown is the hustlers trying to sell knock-off handbags, so steer clear of anyone leading you to Louis Vuitton in an alley. Lunar New Year means lots of celebrations, parades, and crowds, which can be hectic and busy in a fun way. A great Sunday afternoon is early dim sum followed by a foot rub, food for your soul and soles.

1

LAM ZHOU HANDMADE NOODLE

This beloved noodle and dumpling spot has recently relocated to a new space, a nondescript, slightly retro-looking storefront on the Bowery. Aesthetics are not important, not when there are dumplings to be had, because these are truly the best in the city.

This spot is pretty no-frills, but there is beer and an abundance of hot sauces, including chili oil, and that is all you need. The boiled and fried dumplings are equally delicious and impressive in their depth of flavor; you can taste every ingredient and the meat-to-skin ratio is perfect. The dumplings are truly a glorious texture when fried, the skin thin enough to get a solid crunch but thick enough to hold all the filling. They are also extremely satisfying when boiled, with an almost al dente chew. **LAM ZHOU** is less frenetic than other authentic dumpling shops, so feel free to sit and slurp as long as you want.

2 GREAT NEW YORK NOODLETOWN

GREAT NEW YORK NOO-DLETOWN is almost always mentioned when chefs discuss where they eat late-night after their shifts, and the appeal is easy to see, with authentic, filling food available at reasonable prices, and the cover of darkness to mask any less than exemplary hygiene practices. As the name implies, the noodles are great, in any form: thin and floating in a bowl of rich broth, thick and piled high on a plate of beef chow fun, wrapped around a filling to become dumplings. The menu is enormous and the portions are generous, especially for the prices. The roast pork is some of the best in the city, available over rice or on its own, better than the duck that is hanging in all the windows. Great New York Noodletown is small and can be slightly chaotic, so getting food to go might be a better option if they are busy. Cash only.

NOM WAH TEA PARLOR

NOM WAH TEA PARLOR is a special place, open since 1920 on a stretch of Doyers Street formerly known as the "Bloody Angle," because the sharp curve of the street was a frequent site for gang fights. This narrow, picturesque street appears in many movies and TV shows, and the only scuffles likely to happen now are over who gets the last *shumai* at Nom Wah. Nom Wah has the patina of a place with a soul, and recently the younger generation of ownership has taken over, expanded the brand, and simplified operations, without diminishing the feel of authenticity in the air. Dim sum at Nom Wah is an easy introduction to those unfamiliar with the art, because the menu has photos that help you select your dishes. Service is efficient but not cushy. The wait times on weekends can be crushing, but the menu is the same at all times of the day and night, so a weekday lunch or early meal on the weekends is a viable option to avoid the crowds. There are other Nom Wah locations open throughout the city, but nothing beats the experience of the original tea parlor.

4 JING FONG

Dining at **JING FONG** feels much like crashing a Chinese banquet, and sometimes you might actually be doing just that. The dining room is massive, seating 800 people, and is accessed by escalators. The sheer size of the place alleviates some of the wait times, but the entrance area can be quite crowded on weekends. Dining feels much like the dining hall on a cruise ship, with a glorious sense of mad chaos; don't be afraid to wave down that cart of dumplings, or to ask your neighbors what they are eating. True to form, the menu is extremely large, and everything is well executed, which is impressive given the sheer number of options. This is a truly immersive, authentic dim sum experience, with carts serving until 3:30 pm on weekdays and 4 pm on weekends.

5

10BELOW

I scream, you scream, we all scream for ROLLED ice cream! A sweet treat for the Instagram era, watching this ice cream get made is almost as much fun as eating it. These rolled ice cream treats are made in front of you in under two minutes, on a plate that is -10°F, incorporating the fresh ingredients and flavors of your choosing. The end result is smooth, creamy, and damn good looking. The combinations are seemingly endless, and in the winter months the lines can be as well, so keep that in mind when you "roll" on up. **10BELOW** is a glimpse into a more modern side of Chinatown, a reinvention of classic flavors and techniques that feels exciting and new.

THE LOWER EAST SIDE CRAWL

1. **SHOPSIN'S,** INSIDE THE ESSEX STREET MARKET, NEW YORK, 120 ESSEX ST., (917) 907-4506, SHOPSINS.COM

2. **RUSS & DAUGHTERS CAFE,** 127 ORCHARD ST., NEW YORK, (212) 475-4880 EXT. 2, RUSSANDDAUGHTERSCAFE.COM

3. **KATZ'S DELICATESSEN,** 205 E. HOUSTON ST., NEW YORK, (212) 254-2246, KATZSDELICATESSEN.COM

4. **ECONOMY CANDY,** 108 RIVINGTON ST., NEW YORK, (212) 254-1534, ECONOMYCANDY.COM

5. **SUPERMOON BAKEHOUSE,** 120 RIVINGTON ST., NEW YORK, SUPERMOONBAKEHOUSE.COM

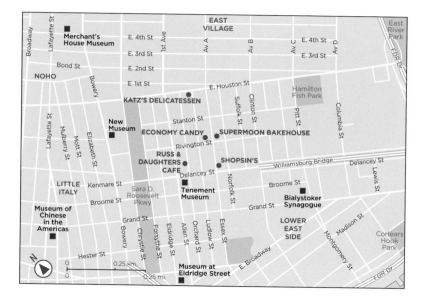

Lower East Side

L.E.S. is More

FOR A LONG TIME, THE LOWER EAST SIDE WAS RICH IN HISTORY ONLY. It's a historically immigrant neighborhood, and historically Jewish, but the last ten years have seen high-end luxury buildings rising next to former tenements and swanky nightlife bringing in hip scenesters looking for fun. The deep immigrant legacy lives on through the culinary offerings; most elements of Jewish cuisine have roots as peasant fare, and now those same ingredients are often incorporated into more upscale dishes. The Lower East Side still feels a little raw and gritty; it maintains a distinct identity from its bordering neighborhoods, and is reminiscent of what the East Village was 25 years ago. Wylie Dufresne was the first chef to make the LES a culinary destination when he opened the groundbreaking 71 Clinton Fresh Food in 1999. Since that time more young and hungry chefs have flocked to the area, making the food scene a true mix of edgy and old-school.

1

SHOPSIN'S

SHOPSIN'S is a truly unique experience, packing a ton of personality, shtick, and flavors into a very small corner of the Essex Street Market. The Essex Street Market is a precursor to all of the upscale food halls that now dot the city, and has been providing the LES with affordable and fresh food for the last 75 years. A wide variety of vendors and specialty products are represented, with everything from Goya pork rinds to artisanal cheese available; this is a market that is meant to serve the needs of the neighborhood, and offers a little piece of home for everyone in the form of food from all over the world. Shopsin's is the only "full service" (just barely) restaurant in the market, and serves what is best described as stoner food. The menu features over 600 items' worth of unique, gut-busting combinations spanning all meals, nationalities, and food types. Shopsin's is not for the faint of heart; legendary owner Ken Shopsin can be gruff and unwelcoming, and if you don't feel comfortable ordering a sandwich called the "JewBoy," then perhaps you should eat elsewhere. The kitchen is remarkably small considering the number of ingredients that must be stocked and the quality of the food that comes out of it. The decor is a random selection of memorabilia, photos, and bits and bobs. There can be long waits, and they are only open until 2 pm, so best to plan ahead.

2 RUSS & DAUGHTERS CAFE

RUSS & DAUGHTERS is the beloved appetizing shop that has been on Houston Street for over one hundred years and four generations of the Russ family. More than bagels and schmears, Russ & Daughters sells some of the finest smoked fish, caviar, baked sweets, and noshes in the city, and they opened the cafe around the corner to expand their offerings in a proper sit-down setting. Comforting like a diner and a hug from your bubby, the space is bright and simple, evocative of an old-school soda shop; the staff in lab coats

is a carryover from the original shop. The food is classic with a little flair; the famous Super Heebster (horseradish dill cream cheese, salmon and whitefish salad, wasabi-flavored roe), which is available at the store on a bagel, made the move but is served open-face on thin bagel crisps. There are big platters with fish and spreads for sharing, caviar, soups, egg dishes, all taking advantage of the famous fish offerings, and sweet options.

3

KATZ'S DELICATESSEN

If you know two things about the LES, make it these two: 1) It's pronounced "House-ton Street," not like the city in Texas, and 2) **KATZ'S DELI** has the best pastrami. In its present location since 1917 and in existence since 1888, Katz's is the most famous deli in New York City, now drawing throngs of tourists to a spot that was initially created to service the blossoming neighborhood. If you have seen *When Harry Met Sally,* you have seen Katz's, but the true vibe must be experienced in person in order to be appreciated, or understood. Katz's can be chaotic and there is no coddling here, but the food is delicious enough to justify their longevity and lack of concern for service. No one cares if you have to wait 30 minutes to get in when there is corned beef and pastrami that has been cured for 30 days. The sandwiches are massive, more than a mouthful and more than a bellyful, but you won't want to share. Latkes, blintzes, hot dogs, all your Jewish deli favorites are here, and even if your boy is not in the army, you can still "send a salami" anywhere in the country, if you want to give your friends at home a taste of the real deal. New York City does not get much more authentic than this, even if the "big sandwich" is not as catchy as the "big apple." N.B.: Katz's is kosher-style. They do serve cheese with meat; they are also open 24 hours.

4

ECONOMY CANDY

ECONOMY CANDY is what children's dreams are made of, a store that is literally filled with candy, floor to ceiling. Since 1937 Economy Candy has been keeping dentists in business with bulk-size packages of everything from jelly beans to imported chocolate treats. Walking into Economy Candy turns everyone into a kid again, the nostalgic innocence of the store is hard to find elsewhere, and it is hard for anyone not to get excited about giant candy bars. For the less sweet-inclined, there are also nuts and dried fruits, but the oversized bags of colorful naughty treats are hard to beat. This place packs a wow factor that must be seen to be believed.

5

SUPERMOON BAKEHOUSE

For a hint of sweet that is more indicative of the "new" LES, check out **SUPERMOON BAKEHOUSE** down the street. This bakery for the food porn set features out-of-this world croissant combinations including cruffins and bi-color filled croissants, and the large glass wall allows a front-row seat to the croissant-making magic. Everything about this spot is clever, from the packaging and decor to the flavor combinations, and the overall effect is authentic, not gimmicky, unlike so many modern sweets shops.

THE TRIBECA CRAWL

1. **BUBBY'S,** 120 HUDSON ST., NEW YORK, (212) 219-0666, BUBBYS.COM

2. **GRAND BANKS,** HUDSON RIVER PARK, PIER 25, NEW YORK, (212) 660-6312, GRANDBANKS.NYC.COM

3. **LOCANDA VERDE,** 377 GREENWICH ST., NEW YORK, (212) 925-3797, LOCANDAVERDE.COM

4. **BRANDY LIBRARY,** 25 N. MOORE ST., NEW YORK, (212) 226-5545, BRANDYLIBRARY.COM

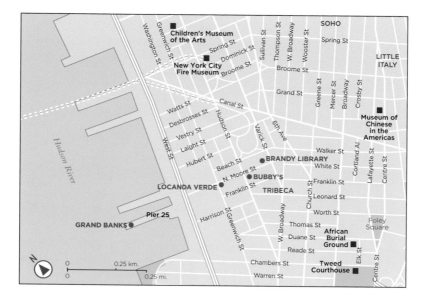

Tribeca

A Neighborhood of Strollers and High Rollers

Yeah, I'm up at Brooklyn, now I'm down in Tribeca
Right next to De Niro, but I'll be hood forever . . .
—Jay-Z, "Empire State of Mind"

TRIBECA, NAMED AS THE TRIANGLE BELOW CANAL STREET, currently has the most expensive home prices in New York City, and it very much feels like a neighborhood, albeit a fancy neighborhood. Cobblestoned streets are lined with former industrial buildings that have been converted to light-filled lofts that attract high-profile actors, artists, and models. A top-notch public school, easy transit options, and waterside parks add to the family-friendly appeal, and have made Tribeca the most coveted zip code for those who can afford to live anywhere they choose. There is no shortage of luxury children's boutiques, and a Tribeca mother is a special species of NYC resident, distinguished by her pin-thin frame and propensity toward athleisure wear, constantly on her way to or coming from an exercise class. The Tribeca Film Festival was started by Robert De Niro and his producing partner Jane Rosenthal in 2002, reportedly to revitalize the neighborhood after the devastation of the 9/11 attacks. Tribeca has attracted high-profile chefs for many years, and continues to have a mix of destination dining and neighborhood spots.

1 BUBBY'S

BUBBY'S is the hot spot for the stroller set, with rows of luxury strollers often lined up outside on the weekends, their tiny occupants inside learning that "B" is for "brunch," and "Bubby's." Bubby's is quintessentially American, and began as a pie shop selling pies to restaurants and residents over 25 years ago and now offers a full menu of breakfast and comfort-food staples.

In addition to the famous pies, southern-leaning items like the flaky biscuits and fried chicken are standouts. There are salads and healthier options to satisfy the Soul Cycle set, and the kids' menu is a virtual paradise for little tummies. Bubby's is an essential Tribeca restaurant, as close to a local diner as the high rents will allow, with a satisfying menu that will hit that spot for any meal of the day, multiple times a week if needed.

2

GRAND BANKS

When the sun shines, you can't get any closer to waterside dining than at **GRAND BANKS**, because you are in the water, open, on a boat. This refurbished wooden schooner parked at Pier 25 in Hudson River Park is the perfect way to spend the afternoon

or evening, sipping rosé or craft cocktails and feasting on oysters among other seasonal, sustainable seafood specialties. The piers along Hudson River Park are perfect for exercising, lying out, or just looking at New Jersey across the river, and a drink or snack at Grand Banks pairs perfectly with all those activities. They take a limited number of reservations daily during their season and encourage most guests to come as walk-ins; just make sure you arrive early to avoid lines, and don't get seasick!

3

LOCANDA VERDE

LOCANDA VERDE is a neighborhood restaurant because it is open for all meals every day, and it is a destination restaurant because they serve some of the best food in the city. Located in the swanky Greenwich Hotel (Robert DeNiro is a co-owner) Locanda Verde serves seasonal Italian food in an inviting and convivial space. Chef and restaurateur Andrew Carmellini's skill is making simple ingredients shine; his whipped ricotta appetizer is akin to tasting the cheese for the first time, and his roast chicken bursts with juicy garlic flavor. Not to be missed are the lamb meatball sliders, which are light and accented with a touch of brine from pickled cucumbers, and any of the house-made pastas. The lemon ricotta pancakes at brunch are worth getting out of bed for. Reserve in advance or take your shot at a bar seat, but be warned. Tribeca residents take their real estate, bar seats and otherwise, very seriously.

4

BRANDY LIBRARY

Tribeca has a number of proper, no-nonsense bars with questionable bathrooms and good jukeboxes, but for something more civilized, head to **BRANDY LIBRARY**. Brandy Library is devoted to all things brandy and brown liquor, with a cocktail menu and spirit list that weighs enough to rival any volume in a library, and amber lighting that makes you feel as if you are actually in a brandy bottle. This is a spot for adult conversation and sipping, not slamming, classic drinks in large leather chairs, and it offers rare vintages and blends that are not found elsewhere. There is a menu of light bites designed to go well with the variety of booze offered. The crowd tends to pull from the banks in the area, as expense accounts are helpful, but it is a one-of-a-kind spot to conjure up some friendly spirits.

THE FINANCIAL DISTRICT CRAWL

1. **DELMONICO'S,** 56 BEAVER ST., NEW YORK, (212) 509-1144, DELMONICOSRESTAURANT.COM

2. **ADRIENNE'S PIZZA BAR,** 54 STONE ST., NEW YORK, (212) 248-3838, ADRIENNESPIZZABARNYC.COM

3. **NOBU,** 195 BROADWAY, NEW YORK, (212) 219-0500, NOBURESTURANTS.COM

4. **TEMPLE COURT BAR,** 5 BEEKMAN ST., NEW YORK, (212) 658-1848, TEMPLECOURTNYC.COM

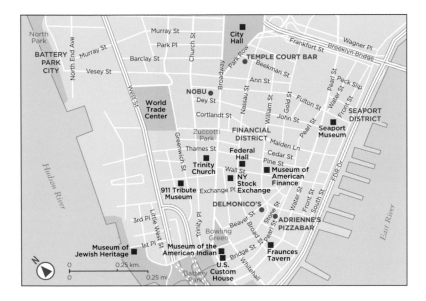

Financial District (FiDi)

No Longer All Work and No Play

THE FINANCIAL DISTRICT HAS A WHOLE NEW ATTITUDE AND A SASSY NEW NAME TO MATCH, FiDi. One of the most historic areas of Manhattan as well as the island's longtime financial hub, FiDi has recently become more of a residential area, luring residents with flashy, amenity-laden buildings and hard-to-beat views. Historically bustling during by day and deserted by night, exciting new restaurant options are taking advantage of the larger base of permanent residents now calling the area home. The shadow of 9/11 still looms large, and the 9/11 Memorial as well as the One World Trade Observatory have become two of the can't-miss sites of the city. Bulls and bears both get hungry, and FiDi is never "short" on fantastic options.

1

DELMONICO'S

Opened in 1837, **DELMONICO'S** predates both the Brooklyn Bridge and the Statue of Liberty, and is responsible for innovating many elements of the American dining experience. Delmonico's is credited as the first restaurant to use printed menus and tablecloths, admit female diners without a male companion, offer a hamburger on a printed menu, and provide a separate wine list. If that is not historically significant enough, Delmonico's is also the birthplace of Eggs Benedict, Baked Alaska, and Lobster Newburg, all of which, along with the signature Delmonico Steak (a beautifully charred boneless rib eye) are still present on the menu. Delmonico's is well preserved and elegant, and dining there feels like an event. The crowd for lunch draws heavily on the area's financial and political movers and shakers, and dinner is more of the same with some tourists. For a more casual option, as an unaccompanied woman or not, there is the Grill Room with a large bar, televisions, and booth seating. Delmonico's has many private rooms, to wheel and deal or celebrate a good day in the market.

2 ADRIENNE'S PIZZA BAR

Stone Street is a charming, blink-and-you-miss-it stretch of cobblestone, surrounded by historic buildings, many of which have been converted to restaurants. During warm months (usually beginning in March) the restaurants and pubs provide outdoor seating, giving the street the feel of a lively block party and providing the perfect spot for employees at the surrounding financial institutions to loosen their ties and tie one on. Stone Street is one of the city's oldest streets, and many of the buildings are protected by the City's Landmark Preservation Commission, which allows this former back alley to stand in stark contrast to the cold skyscrapers throughout the rest of the area. **ADRIENNE'S** draws a huge crowd for lunch and dinner, and one taste of their signature square pies, served on a perfect-for-sharing 18½-inch tray and you will see why. The toppings are straightforward, and the texture of the pizza is unique and utterly satisfying, ideal for a well-deserved lunch break or as the start of a night out. The interior of Adrienne's is simple and casual, and the salads, baked dishes, and pastas available mean that nearby residents never need to wonder where to order in from.

3

NOBU

NOBU has not been unique to New York for quite some time, but the new New York City flagship will remind you why the formula has proven to be so successful, and why they command the prices they do. The setting is dramatic and beautiful.

The upstairs bar/lounge area has breathtaking ceiling height and an eye-catching central bar from which the rest of the room seems to radiate. Bar seating is first come, first served, but if you innocently try to take a lounge seat you will most likely be told they are reserved; some things never change. The lack of change on the menu, however, is a good thing, because there is nothing better than Nobu's signature dishes, including the yellowtail jalapeño (they were the first) and the sashimi New Style (seared with hot sesame oil.) There are cooked dishes (the famous rock shrimp tempura, black cod with miso in butter lettuce) as well as dishes with meat, veggies, etc, so even the non-fish eaters will find something that is sure to satisfy. The downstairs dining room is separated into two areas, one being covered in erector-set-like branches of light wood,

and a darker area set under the staircase; there is also sushi-bar seating. This Nobu feels chic and relevant, the embodiment of all that is new and fashionable downtown.

4 TEMPLE COURT BAR

The lobby of the Beekman Hotel, where the **TEMPLE COURT BAR** is located, has become Instagram famous for the upward-looking view from the atrium, where the floors rise to the sky around you, but the view from the ground is pretty impressive as well. The Temple Court is the Tom Colicchio–helmed restaurant in the hotel, which also houses the Keith McNally–conceived Augustine. The Temple Court Bar looks set-design perfect, with every piece of furniture, glassware, and knick-knack seemingly sourced from some sort of early-1900s period drama. There is a proper dining room as well, but the spot to be is the lounge area or at the beautifully lit bar, where retro cocktails and bites sized from small to large are available. The vibe is sophisticated and retro-glam, and since it is in a hotel, the spot is open throughout the whole day, from morning coffee to nightcap.

THE WILLIAMSBURG CRAWL

1. **PETER LUGER STEAKHOUSE,** 178 BROADWAY, BROOKLYN, (718) 387-7400, PETERLUGER.COM

2. **EMMY SQUARED,** 364 GRAND ST., BROOKLYN, (718) 360-4535, EMMYSQUAREDBK.COM

3. **LILIA,** 567 UNION AVE., BROOKLYN, (718) 576-3095, LILIANEWYORK.COM

4. **THE COMMODORE,** 366 METROPOLITAN AVE., BROOKLYN, (718) 218-7632

5. **MAISON PREMIERE,** 298 BEDFORD AVE., BROOKLYN, (347) 335-0446, MAISONPREMIERE.COM

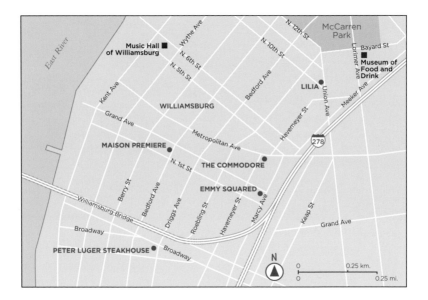

Williamsburg

Eat like a Hipster

WILLIAMSBURG IS SO HIP IT HURTS; Williamsburg embraces everything quirky and creative and counterculture, and is stereotyped as hipster heaven. The commitment to sourcing artisan items and ironically adopting esoteric bits of mainstream pop culture leads to some truly unique stores and restaurants in the area. From April to October, Smorgasburg hosts Saturdays in Williamsburg, on the Williamsburg waterfront, which is an all-star open-air food market that has propelled many food trucks and small businesses to the forefront of pop culture. Williamsburg is ground zero for exploring and celebrating funky, one-of-a-kind spots that have all but disappeared in Manhattan.

1 PETER LUGER STEAKHOUSE

PETER LUGER is old Williamsburg, and old-school. Established in 1887, Peter Luger is arguably the most famous steakhouse in New York City, if not the country. Eating at Luger's on a visit to New York is a rite of passage, and you never forget your first Luger's steak (neither do your arteries). The list of offerings at Luger's is not large, and the signature dish is USDA Prime porterhouse for one to four people; all of the other steakhouse food groups are represented, including thick-cut bacon, wedge salad, shrimp cocktail, and potatoes in many forms. The interior is reminiscent of a German beer hall, and the well-worn wood speaks to the heritage of the restaurant. If you wish to experience Luger's and not burst all of your buttons, the way to do it is to go for lunch, when they offer the Luger burger, a half-pound beauty that can be topped with their famous bacon. Luger's has rules and can afford to not care whom they offend; reservations are required and they do not accept credit cards; cash, check, debit card, or Luger's card are the only acceptable methods of payment. The Peter Luger experience has spawned a million imitators, but there is nothing quite like the real thing.

 EMMY SQUARED

New Yorkers take great pride in their pizza, so imagine the waves caused when a restaurant dedicated to Detroit-style pizza debuted, and it won the hearts of critics and diners alike. Detroit pizza is defined by its square shape and thick, cheesy crust. The reason for the square shape of Detroit pizza is tied to Detroit's (other) most famous product: automobiles. Detroit pizza is baked in a tray that was originally intended to hold industrial auto parts, traditionally made of blue steel. The pan and cooking method give the pizza its signature deep-dish form and crunchy crust, which gets an extra bite from the cheese that melts onto the crust. The center of the pizza however remains chewy, offering a perfect contrast to the crust, but corner pieces

are still the most coveted. **EMMY SQUARED** offers a wide range of composed pizzas; The Emmy, with mozzarella, banana peppers, onions, ranch dressing, and a side of sauce, is an Instagram favorite, and the pizza with vodka sauce is the pizza tweak you never knew you needed. Emmy also serves a decadent burger, Le Big Matt (so named for co-owner Matthew Hyland), and crispy cheese curds that put mozzarella sticks to shame. Emmy Squared has become quite the destination (the power of the Internet), so reserve in advance if possible.

3

LILIA

Missy Robbins was the girl power behind restaurants that did not bear her name, and with the launch of **LILIA** a few years ago she has quickly cemented her well-deserved spot on the chef food chain. You may wonder why such an accomplished chef who once helmed the kitchen of the now-defunct A Voce in the high-rent mall that is the Time Warner Center would want to open in Brooklyn, but once you dine at Lilia you realize why choosing Williamsburg makes sense. Lilia physically feels like a departure from Manhattan and any sort

of pretense or sense of urgency, a place with a slower pace churning out dishes that exhibit a delicacy and balance of flavors that take time and skill. Everything you eat at Lilia demonstrates a superior attention to detail, especially the pastas, which are often visually and texturally impressive. Lilia Caffè offers savory and sweet pastries, panini, and coffee throughout the day.

4 THE COMMODORE

THE COMMODORE is pure Williamsburg: a purposely divey bar with video games and frozen drinks that happens to serve some of the best fried chicken around. Hit up The Commodore early in the evening, to avoid crowds of over-served and over-entitled youngsters and to give your body a chance to recover from the fatty deliciousness that you fed it. The best dish is a plate of fried chicken thighs and small biscuits, thanks to a Pies 'n' Thighs alum in the kitchen; best to wipe your fingers off after you lick them clean and before you head to the video games. It can be hard to find a place to perch to eat your food, so be prepared to throw some elbows before you eat your thighs.

5

MAISON PREMIERE

Stepping into **MAISON PREMIERE** is like stepping back in time to old New Orleans, to a slower pace, where lingering is encouraged. Once inside, everywhere you look is beautiful, and if cocktails and raw bars are your thing, then you have found your new favorite spot. Oyster Happy Hour draws big crowds,

and the uniquely flavored mignonettes are served in little droppers. When weather allows, there's a pretty patio out back; you can also get cozy inside at a table or saddle up to the large horseshoe bar. The cocktails here are crafted but not pretentious, and earned Maison Premiere a James Beard Award for Outstanding Cocktail Program. If you're feeling brave, try out one of their premium bottles of absinthe and wish for the best—just hope the little green fairy leads you back home.

THE DUMBO CRAWL

1. **LUKE'S LOBSTER,** 11 WATER ST., NEW YORK, (917) 882-7516, ,
    LUKESLOBSTER.COM

2. **CECCONI'S,** 55 WATER ST., NEW YORK, (718)650-3900,
    CECCONISDUMBO.COM

3. **THE RIVER CAFÉ,** 1 WATER ST., NEW YORK, (718) 522-5200,
    RIVERCAFE.COM

4. **1 HOTEL,** 60 FURMAN ST., NEW YORK, (877) 803-1111, 1HOTELS.COM

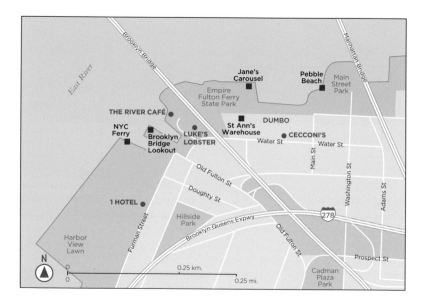

DUMBO

Views and Chews

DUMBO (DOWN UNDER MANHATTAN BRIDGE OVERPASS, nothing to do with a flying elephant) is easily accessed by walking across the Brooklyn Bridge. Once you arrive, your reward is being treated to some of most breathtaking views of Manhattan, which you just left. These views, and converted warehouse luxury lofts, have been attracting well-heeled residents for the past decade, but a slew of new buildings, a hip new hotel, and new waterfront attractions have recently brought the neighborhood more attention than ever before. On nice days Brooklyn Bridge Park can't be beat for views and general urban outdoorsiness, and Jane's carousel, a century-old restored carousel enclosed in glass, is a beautiful juxtaposition with the modernity of the Manhattan skyline behind it. Photo op: Washington Street between Front and Water has become a huge photo attraction as it captures the cobblestone streets, the Manhattan Bridge, and the Empire State Building. Shopping is mainly concentrated around the Empire Stores, which used to be a tobacco warehouse, but now just has smokin' retail and food options like a West Elm, the F.E.E.D Cafe, and Cecconi's.

1

LUKE'S LOBSTER

What is better than eating a lobster roll with a view of the water? Nothing! The Dumbo waterfront is not the coast of Maine, but the lobsters you are eating were caught there, responsibly. **LUKE'S** is a successful mini-chain with several outposts throughout the country but the DUMBO location, right on the East River, is by far the most fun, located in the historic smokestack building directly under the bridge. Grab a lobster or crab roll and walk around to check out the neighborhood, just don't get too carried away and try to jump into the river . . .

2 CECCONI'S

CECCONI'S DUMBO is the New York outpost of the swishy Italian eatery from London that is also in Los Angeles and Miami. Housed in Empire Stores, Cecconi's has prime bridge views and outside seating right on the waterfront promenade, making it the ideal spot to sip and be seen on nice days. The Italian fare is straightforward and best when accompanied by an Aperol spritz. There is lounge seating, bar seating, and proper tables when dining inside, and the bar area is especially lively during happy hour. This is where the hip set is hunkering down in DUMBO, and that will only increase when Soho House opens upstairs.

3

THE RIVER CAFÉ

THE RIVER CAFÉ is transporting, a place for special occasions, even if you are just celebrating it being the end of the week. Nestled back on its own piece of waterfront, you are greeted with pristine landscaping and abundant flowers as you enter and make your way to the dining room, whose focal point is a huge wall of windows. The view is simply breathtaking, and it underscores the entire dining experience with a sense of enchantment under the gaze of Lady Liberty. The food is classic American, with a focus on high-quality seasonal ingredients. The River Café recently celebrated its 40th anniversary, and is back and better than ever after facing destruction from Hurricane Sandy. Jackets are required.

4

1 HOTEL

Well hello there, aren't you pretty? Luxurious and environmentally conscious, **1 HOTEL** fits in perfectly in Brooklyn. The open-air 1 Rooftop bar boasts the rarest of city features, a plunge pool, which is only available for hotel guests but visually pleasing nonetheless. The priceless view makes you feel like Lady Liberty is your wingwoman, making 1 Rooftop one of the hottest new spots in Brooklyn or Manhattan. There are bites available if you need to soak up more than the views. The Hotel also features the Brooklyn Heights Social Club, a modern update on a social club with craft cocktails and a chic, cozy aesthetic and the same commitment to sustainability. Environmental consciousness has never looked so sexy, and you will want to look your best as well.

THE HARLEM CRAWL

1. **SYLVIA'S,** 328 MALCOLM X BLVD., NEW YORK, (212) 996-0660, SYLVIASRESTAURANT.COM

2. **RED ROOSTER,** 310 LENOX AVE., NEW YORK, (212) 792-9001, REDROOSTERHARLEM.COM

3. **HAJII'S, AKA BLUE LINE DELI,** 2135 1ST AVE., NEW YORK, (646) 682-7482

4. **DINOSAUR BAR-B-QUE,** 700 W. 125TH ST., NEW YORK, (212) 694-1777, DINOSAURBARBQUE.COM/LOCATION/HARLEM

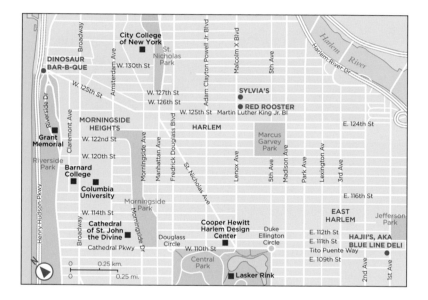

Harlem

Keeping it Real

HARLEM HAS BEEN CONSIDERED A BLACK CULTURAL MECCA since the early 20th century, when some of the most seminal works of African-American literature, music, and theater were created in the neighborhood. The Harlem Renaissance of that time produced lasting legacies of artistic expression from Harlem figures such as Langston Hughes, Duke Ellington, Louis Armstrong, and many others, solidifying Harlem's place in history as the most influential hub of African-American culture in the country. The national spotlight was also cast on Harlem during the unrest of the Civil Rights Movement, as religious and political figures like Malcom X and Adam Clayton Powell Jr. rose to prominence to provide voices for the oppressed.

The famous Apollo Theater still stands as a reminder of Harlem's glory days and the vibrancy of this neighborhood. The Harlem of today, however, is a neighborhood in transition, caught between honoring its culturally significant past and the residents that made it possible, and the ever-present threat of gentrification. The food in Harlem is as rich with history as flavor, paying homage to where the original residents came from (the South, the Caribbean) and the lifestyle and tastes of the modern Harlem resident. Dining in Harlem provides a glimpse of the history of the neighborhood as well as its future.

1

SYLVIA'S

SYLVIA'S is a Harlem institution, a stalwart of Southern cuisine in a neighborhood whose landscape is constantly changing. People may claim that it's touristy, which is not entirely fair, but going to Harlem without checking out Sylvia's is like a trip to Orlando without visiting Disney World—you just need to have the experience. Sylvia's offers top-notch Southern comfort food in a welcoming and lively environment, enhanced by the soundtrack of head bobbing hip-hop and R&B, and a live gospel brunch on Sundays. Every meal starts with a basket of homemade cornbread, sweet and spongy and ready to soak up

all the gravies and special "sassy" sauces to come; pair it with a sweet tea. While the chicken and waffles are extremely popular, the combo to get is the fried chicken and ribs, which comes with two sides. The chicken (choose white meat or dark meat) is just as it should be—crunchy on the outside and moist on the inside, and the ribs are tender, doused in the aforementioned Sassy Sauce. Mac 'n' cheese and mashed potatoes are two of the top sides, although it's hard to go wrong. Dessert is not to be missed, and breakfast is also served most days. Sylvia's will fill your belly and your soul.

2 RED ROOSTER

While Sylvia's represents the history of Harlem and is an homage to family recipes from the South, **RED ROOSTER** is a sexy representation of the Harlem of today. Red Rooster feels alive and bursting with energy and style, the vibe enhanced by the always-cool music and colorful artwork. Going to Red Rooster feels like an event, and the patrons tend to dress accordingly, making it one of the most fashionable places in the neighborhood. Red Rooster is helmed by Marcus Samuelsson, a Harlem resident. It is part of the mission of the Red Rooster to give back to the neighborhood by making an effort to hire from the neighborhood and support local musicians and artists, as well as offering neighborhood cooking classes. Red Rooster is named for a legendary Harlem speakeasy, and it keeps that legacy alive with Ginny's Supper Club downstairs, offering dinner, drinks, and live music in a sensual atmosphere. Like the rest of the vibe, the food at Red Rooster is bold and exciting, and doesn't take itself too seriously. Red Rooster has an intrinsic coolness that can only be understood by experiencing it firsthand.

3

HAJII'S, AKA BLUE LINE DELI

Bodegas are a uniquely New York City phenomenon, a one-stop shop for assorted grocery items, energy drinks, and high-quality grill work. A bacon, egg, and cheese sandwich is never better than when from the corner bodega, a foil-wrapped cure for a long night or a long day and usually under $4. With bodegas it is best not to look too closely; cats are often insurance against rodent intruders and the lettuce is a little wilted, but there is nothing more New York than grabbing a sandwich from your local bodega and knowing it will be exactly what you expect. It is fitting that the legend of the chopped cheese most likely has its origins in a bodega, and quite possibly this bodega, **HAJII'S**, or the **BLUE LINE DELI**. Largely under the radar for many Manhattanites, the chopped cheese is considered the New York City answer to the Philly cheesesteak, and although delicious, is best procured from bodegas with dubious culinary credibility. A chopped cheese is the following: hamburger meat, chopped up with a spatula on a flat-top grill, covered in cheese, topped with lettuce, tomato, onions, ketchup, and mayo on a roll or hero. This is a New York sandwich for real New Yorkers, and fans who grew up with this food will never accept any fancy, dressed-up, name-brand version of the sandwich. Hajii's is a place for the neighborhood and only attracts outsiders seeking to experience the real-deal chopped cheese; although this is the ideal drunk food, we recommend going during the day if it is your first time.

4 DINOSAUR BAR-B-QUE

DINOSAUR BAR-B-QUE did not originate in Harlem, but since its arrival in 2004, it has become a go-to spot in the neighborhood for everyone from families to leather-clad bikers. This outlet of a mini-chain originally from upstate New York is massive, housed in a former meatpacking plant on the far West Side, close to the famous Cotton Club. The decor feels more Southern "themed" and in your face than Sylvia's, but when their pulled pork is in your face nothing else matters. Any time of day or night, Dinosaur is rocking, so it is best to reserve if possible; they offer a happy hour deal during the week and live music later on weekend evenings.

All of the hickory-smoked meats are juicy and full of smoky goodness, especially the brisket; there are some less traditional options such as BBQ Salmon jerky, but, the best move is to stick with heaping piles of meat and naughty, decadent sides.

THE RED HOOK CRAWL

1. **HOMETOWN BAR-B-QUE,** 454 VAN BRUNT ST., BROOKLYN, (347) 294-4644, HOMETOWNBBQUE.COM

2. **DEFONTES,** 379 COLUMBIA ST., BROOKLYN, (718) 625-8052, DEFONTESOFBROOKLYN.COM

3. **VAN BRUNT STILLHOUSE,** 6 BAY ST., BROOKLYN, (718) 852-6405, VANBRUNTSTILLHOUSE.COM

4. **BROOKLYN CRAB,** 24 REED ST., BROOKLYN, (718) 643-2722, BROOKLYNCRAB.COM

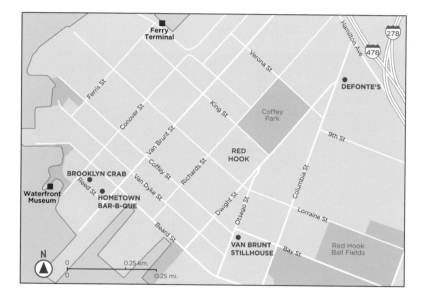

Red Hook

The Next Big Thing

RED HOOK IS THE NEXT NEXT BIG THING. While it may feel out of the way, you can easily get there on the water taxi which makes the adventure even more fun.

Red Hook, "hooking" out into the East River, was once one of the busiest ports in the country. Originally home to thousands of dock workers, Red Hook was historically riddled with crime and rough around the edges: It was home to lots of wise guys, including Al Capone and several "waste management" companies. In the past 20 years, much has been done to revive the neighborhood and waterfront; however, the strong sense of community is still unchanged. There are delicious restaurants, no BS bars, and a slew of unique small businesses (and some large, like IKEA), which makes the area feel more like you're in a small town upstate rather than mere miles from Manhattan. This crawl is best on a nice day to take advantage of the many outdoor options as well water transportation from Manhattan.

1

HOMETOWN BAR-B-QUE

Your first stop in Red Hook must be **HOMETOWN BAR-B-QUE**. Get there as early as you can to avoid any lines, and use the time spent waiting to narrow down your choices. Hometown is by far the best, most authentic, and inspired BBQ in all of New York City, in large part because of the meticulous and creative mind of Billy Durney. Billy incorporates classic smoking techniques with flavors inspired by items that are classically New York (Katz's pastrami is the inspiration behind his pastrami bacon), and the results are out of this world. Even things you might never consider ordering at a BBQ joint will blow your mind, including the lamb belly *banh mi* and the wood-fired chicken with salsa verde. This place alone is worth the trip, and it is close to the water taxi.

2 DEFONTE'S

DEFONTE'S has been feeding hungry Brooklynites (and more) since the 1920s. Their sandwiches are huge—in variety and size—so if you are unsure order the small, which can still easily feed two. It's almost impossible to make a bad decision here, and they are open for breakfast, serving the potato, egg, and cheese sandwich of your dreams. The Giuseppe Special—eggplant parmigiana, meatball, and melted mozzarella—is righteous, as is the Steak Pizzaiola (usually a special). If you're looking for something cold (and hot), Defonte's serves a perfect version of an Italian Special with hot peppers; many of the sandwiches are served with fried eggplant on them for a unique twist. These are two-handed sandwiches, so put your phone down.

3

VAN BRUNT STILLHOUSE

This artisanal distillery on an otherwise quiet Red Hook street is a great spot to recoup and warm up. The distillery originated when the founder bought a still on Ebay and decided to try to make whiskey. He built the distillery from the ground up with help from his partners and friends, and he sources the wheat, rye, and corn used in their spirits locally from farms upstate. Much of the portfolio has won awards, and you can taste the spirits, including special small-batch/limited releases and craft cocktails, in the comfortable tasting room on weekends. Tours are available; call to inquire.

4 BROOKLYN CRAB

You won't be crabby at this large, indoor/outdoor crab "shack," spread over two levels across from Fairway and the river. Feast on fresh, sustainable seafood while you challenge your friends (or kiddies) to mini golf, cornhole, and bocce. Tables are usually snapped up quickly, but there's a huge bar and lots of room to spread out and play to pass the time. Raw bar, buckets of crabs, and cocktails in plastic cups are the go-tos here, but don't miss sunset over the water from one of their two decks overlooking the harbor.

THE FOOD HALLS / MARKETS CRAWL

1. **CHELSEA MARKET,** 75 9TH AVE., NEW YORK, (212) 652-2121,
   CHELSEAMARKET.COM

2. **DEKALB MARKET HALL,** 445 ALBEE SQUARE W., BROOKLYN,
   (929) 359-6555, DEKALBMARKETHALL.COM

3. **EATALY FLATIRON,** 200 5TH AVE., NEW YORK, (212) 229-2560,
   EATALY.COM/US_EN/STORES/NYC-FLATIRON

4. **LE DISTRICT,** 225 LIBERTY ST., NEW YORK, (212)981-8588, LEDISTRICT.COM

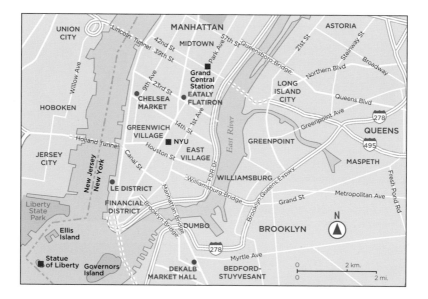

Food Halls / Markets

One-Stop Foodie Shops

SUBURBAN MALLS HAVE FOOD COURTS, and New York City has food halls, the urban equivalent for one-stop eating. Short of a trip to EPCOT, there is no easier way to sample cuisines and foods from various countries that would not naturally overlap. Food halls can seem overwhelming in their offerings, with shopping, fast-casual dining, and proper restaurants all under one roof. In a multi-tasking city like New York, however, this is very convenient. Some food halls are dedicated to only one type of cuisine, exploring all regions and specialties in depth, while others have a random scattering of tasty stalls with no apparent theme or organization. The markets and food halls also host a variety of food- and wine-centric classes, which are especially appealing to New Yorkers, who sometimes forget what it is like to cook in a full-size kitchen.

1

CHELSEA MARKET

CHELSEA MARKET is the mothership of all food halls. It is unclear if anyone has ever eaten at all 35-plus vendors in one day, or if it would even be possible, but that doesn't stop people from trying. Chelsea Market has attracted over 6 million visitors since 1997 and established itself as a tourist destination as well as a neighborhood staple. There are endless eat-in options, grab-and-go shops, and an Anthropologie in case you get dirty and need to buy a cute new top. Some standouts: Los Tacos No. 1 is regarded as making some of the best, most authentic tacos in the city. The Lobster Place is a one-stop shop for everything fish and seafood related, whether you want to eat there or cook at home later. You'll find everything from sushi to lobster rolls and seafood gumbo. They also offer a one-pot lobster boil that is the quickest way to bring New England into your kitchen. Dizengoff is Michael Solomonov's hummus stall, serving fresh, authentic hummus with rotating seasonal toppings, as well as shakshuka, all day. Under the market is the Tippler, a speakeasy-type bar with light bites and craft cocktails. Buddakan and Morimoto are technically located within the Chelsea Market building, if you are inclined to stay for the entire day.

> ### FUN FACT
>
> Chelsea Market is located in the former National Biscuit Co. (Nabisco) Building, where the Oreo was invented. The central fountain was created using discarded drill bits and pipes from the factory.

2 DEKALB MARKET HALL

DEKALB MARKET HALL appears to be completely without plan or theme beyond, "Hey, here is a delicious place to eat." Composed of 40 vendors scattered about a large subterranean space, you are able to wander and stumble upon authentic jerk chicken next to a stand featuring a grandma hand-making pierogies. DeKalb offers many lesser- known vendors as well as second outposts of more established venues, and two large, full-service restaurants, Han Dynasty and Forina. This allows visitors the simultaneous thrill of visiting a famous place as well as discovering a small gem. The biggest draw is an outpost of Katz's deli, offering the signature pastrami, if not the surly service and iconic atmosphere. Hard Times Sundaes, originally a food truck, offers one of the best roadside-style burgers in the city and should not be missed; also worth a visit is an outpost of Lioni Italian Sandwiches, where everything is big—big menu (over 150 items), big sandwiches, big flavors, big muscles on the servers. The sandwiches are all authentic Brooklyn Ital, and the bread is a wonder, soft but strong enough to handle all of the meat piled on. There is no retail component to DeKalb; every stall is for eating, and seating is scarce. The brightly painted walls make ideal backgrounds for getting a picture of the seemingly made-for-Instagram churro ice cream sandwiches.

3 EATALY FLATIRON

A trip to **EATALY** is like a trip to Italy, but with a Metrocard rather than a passport. Eataly allows you to enjoy all of the Italian necessities from breads to balsamico to *burrata* to branzino for a literal taste of La Dolce Vita. The original New York City location in the Flatiron area is a massive, winding labyrinth of high-quality items of every variety and from every region in Italy, all sold in designated areas. It is paradise for cooks and non-cooks alike, with restaurants part of the mix as well; you can have the Agnolotti del Plin at La Pizza & La Pasta, and

then pick up half a pound on the way out. Eataly has everything from the perfect pasta strainer to small-batch extra-virgin olive oil and artfully topped focaccias. There is a strong focus on education as well, with cooking classes and scheduled tastings on offer, and often all of the restaurants offer monthly specials highlighting specific areas of Italy. Eataly is often very crowded and navigating with a grocery basket can be slightly hectic, but it is nothing compared to the crowds at Rome's Spanish Steps in August. The homemade mozzarella is one of the best in New York City, and not to be missed.

4 LE DISTRICT

Ooh la la, **LE DISTRICT** is a little piece of the Seine right on the Hudson, a bustling Francophile's dream inside Brookfield Place. Much like the arrondissements of Paris, Le District is divided into four districts: the Market District, the Café District, the Garden District, and the Restaurant District. The Market District has everything you need to stock up on French specialties including a boulangerie, charcuterie, fromagerie, and imported name-brand French packaged goods. Café District serves coffee and traditional French pastries and other baked goods, as well as chocolate and biscuits from renowned French

confectionery La Cure Gourmande. The Garden District is where to head to cancel out the guilty pleasures of the two districts, offering fresh produce, a juice bar, a salad bar, and grab-and-go fare. The four dining options include intimate Michelin-starred L'Appart; Beaubourg, the brasserie with the happening outdoor terrace; Le Bar, which offers le bites and le drinks with le view; and Bar à Vin, in the center of the market, with more than 30 wines by the glass and almost as many food options to pair with them. Le District is an immersive French experience: no translator required.

THE ARTHUR AVENUE CRAWL

1. **ENZO'S,** 2339 ARTHUR AVE., BRONX, (718) 733-4455, ENZOSBRONXRESTAURANT.COM

2. **RANDAZZO'S,** 2327 ARTHUR AVE., BRONX, (718) 367-4139, RANDAZZOSEAFOOD.COM

3. **CALANDRA'S CHEESE,** 2314 ARTHUR AVE., BRONX, (718) 365-7572, CALANDRASCHEESE.COM

4. **CALABRIA PORK STORE,** 2338 ARTHUR AVE., BRONX, (718) 367-5145

5. **MADONIA BROTHERS BAKERY,** 2348 ARTHUR AVE., BRONX, (718) 295-5573

6. **CASA DELLA MOZZARELLA,** 604 E. 187TH ST., BRONX, (718) 364-1867

7. **BORGATTI'S RAVIOLI & EGG NOODLES,** 632 E. 187TH ST., BRONX, (718) 367-3799, BORGATTIS.COM

8. **ARTHUR AVENUE MARKET,** 2344 ARTHUR AVE., BRONX, (718) 220-0346

9. **TRA DI NOI,** 622 E. 187TH ST., (718) 295-1784, TRADINOI.COM

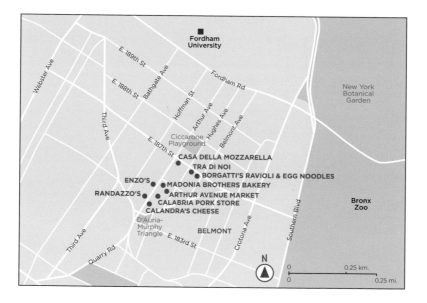

Arthur Avenue

The Real Little Italy

ALL THE GOODFELLAS AND LADIES KNOW THAT ARTHUR AVE-
NUE HAS THE BEST ITALIAN RESTAURANTS, markets, bakeries,
and specialty stores. Located in the Belmont section of the Bronx,
the area around Arthur Avenue and 187th Street is often referred to
as the "real Little Italy," and is the intersection of years of tradition
and generations of families. Arthur Avenue has more family-run
businesses operating for over 100 years than any other part of
the city, and although many of these businesses thrive because of
the local residents, over 85 percent of customers come from more
than five miles away. The authenticity available cannot be rivaled;
many of the shops import hard-to-find items from Italy, and even
if two stores specialize in the same item (cheese, for example),
they will each offer something that the other does not. There is a
strong sense of community, everyone seems to know each other,
and everyone is connected to their strong Italian heritage.

The restaurants and markets are sprinkled over a few blocks,
and it is not hard to make a day of shopping and eating. Going for
lunch, visiting all the stores to stock up on supplies, then staying
for an early dinner is a perfect way to spend an afternoon. An easy
way to get to Arthur Avenue is by taking the Metro North Harlem
Line to Fordham Station (roughly 17 minutes from Grand Central)
and walking for 10 minutes. A visit to Arthur Avenue can be com-
bined with a trip to the New York Botanical Garden or the Bronx
Zoo, just don't let the tigers get a whiff of that mozz. . . . N.B.: Many
of the stores close early, so plan accordingly.

1

ENZO'S

Red sauce is boss at this neighborhood institution that is a perfect place to soak in the flavor of the neighborhood; dining here feels like you are part of the family, and you will be treated as such. The portions are massive and so are the personalities, the crowd a mix of true locals and tourists making the pilgrimage for parmigiana. And what a chicken parmigiana it is—pounded thin, crispy, and covered in the proper proportions of sauce and cheese, this is the perfect example of this dish. All of the old-school staples are here—clams oreganata, fried calamari, meatballs, everything you wish your grandmother made. Reservations and credit cards are accepted, but leaving hungry is not.

RANDAZZO'S

One of the two top seafood spots in the neighborhood, with the freshest fish available, both familiar and exotic. Warm months have fresh shucked oysters and clams for sale on the sidewalk.

3

CALANDRA'S CHEESE

This dairy dynamo is not to be missed. Whether your cheese of choice is cow, sheep, local, or imported, **CALANDRA'S** has it all. There is no need to play coy around the abundant free cheese samples—the friendly staff encourages nibbling as you shop and will help narrow down your selections. Calandra's *burrata* is out of this world, and a relative bargain. Don't miss the lesser-known *burrino*, with a more distinctive rind and roots in Southern Italy. Be warned that the *fior di latte* mozzarella should be ordered a day in advance. Calandra's makes their ricotta and mozzarella fresh daily, and stocks every Italian deli essential in the most authentic way possible. Calandra's Cheese also makes gift boxes to order—a perfect, unique, customizable gift for anyone who appreciates true New York, Italian food, or just simply great cheese.

The free samples might lure you in, but the variety of pasta, cooked and cured meats, and more will fill your table and keep you coming back.

CALABRIA PORK STORE

4 The ultimate hog heaven, **CALABRIA** literally has a sausage chandelier, their entire ceiling covered in hanging sausages. Try all sorts of prosciutto, *sopressata*, and *porchetta* on their own or in any combination with cheese on a sandwich, and don't forget the stuffed peppers.

5 MADONIA BROTHERS BAKERY

This bakery has been family run for three generations, and legend has it the original owner's son was born on the floor of bakery, after a car crashed through the window and scared the mother into labor. Besides keeping newborn babies warm, their ovens churn out the best savory breads, cookies, and cannolis around.

6 CASA DELLA MOZZARELLA

Who makes the best mozzarella on Arthur Avenue is often debated, but the New York Yankees have cast their vote: **CASA DE MOZZARELLA** has been named the official cheese of the Bronx Bombers. This emporium to all things mozzarella makes fresh cheese on premises constantly throughout the day, and supplies the cheese to many of the restaurants in the area. Try it on its own or on a sandwich.

7 BORGATTI'S RAVIOLI & EGG NOODLES

THE place for ravioli; you only have to decide if you want large or small size, and which flavor.

FUNGHI
PORCINI
SECCHI
VALTARO
(PARMA)

8 ARTHUR AVENUE MARKET

The **ARTHUR AVENUE MARKET** was established by Mayor LaGuardia in 1940 as a central indoor place for all of the pushcart vendors to sell their wares. Today it is a bustling hub stocked with every Italian delicacy and prepared food, courtesy of an assortment of vendors all under one roof. Be sure to hit up Mike's Deli for one of their epic sandwiches, including their eggplant parm, which beat Bobby Flay on the Food Network.

9 TRA DI NOI

For a more refined, cozy and quiet dining experience, **TRA DI NOI** is the perfect spot. Italian-born Chef Marco has over 50 years of cooking experience, (he is rumored to have been Sophia Loren's personal chef) and tends to every dish himself to this day. You can taste his keen attention to delicate details, such as the light sheets of pasta in the famous lasagne bolognese. The specials change daily based on what is fresh and available, making this spot especially popular with locals.

THE FLUSHING CRAWL

1. **KUNG FU XIAO LONG BAO,** 59-16 MAIN ST., FLUSHING, (718) 661-2882, KUNGFUXIAOLONGBAO.COM

2. **GOLDEN SHOPPING MALL: TIANJIN DUMPLING HOUSE, LAN ZHOU,** 41-26 MAIN ST., FLUSHING, (917) 478-4536

3. **JOE'S STEAMED RICE ROLLS,** 136-21 ROOSEVELT AVE., FLUSHING, (646) 203-7380

4. **WHITE BEAR,** 135-02 ROOSEVELT AVE., FLUSHING, (718) 961-2322

5. **SZECHUAN HOUSE,** 133-47 ROOSEVELT AVE., FLUSHING, (718)762-2664

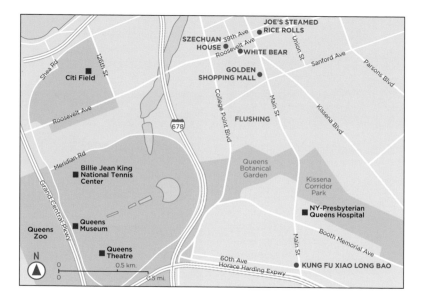

Flushing

Dumpling Crawl

GRAB YOUR CASH AND YOUR APPETITE, and get ready to explore the second largest Chinatown in New York City. Accessible by riding the 7 train until the end or hopping on the Long Island Railroad (faster if a little more expensive), Flushing has a feeling all its own, and some of the best and most affordable Asian eats in the city. The local community is predominantly Korean and Chinese, and the Asian influence in Flushing is obvious, with many signs in Chinese and markets and stores with offerings not widely available elsewhere in New York City. Although some of these restaurants have gained popularity, many are very small and not intended to cater to tourists, meaning that English is not always spoken and bathrooms might not be available, so plan ahead and perhaps pack some Wet-Naps.

1

KUNG FU XIAO LONG BAO

KUNG FU XLB is a little farther away from mass transit and the rest of the places on the crawl, so it should be fit in either in the beginning or the end. But even if you have to walk the half mile from the train, it is not to be missed. Hands down, these *xiao long bao* (soup dumplings) are among the best anywhere in New York. The skin is thin and translucent, and every ingredient is quite pronounced, including some great ginger flavor in the pork variety; there is a perfect amount of soup, aiding in the never glamorous process of successfully slurping a soup dumpling. The crab XLB are not overly fishy, delivering just the right amount of seafood saltiness. They come six in an order and are only $6.50, meaning they won't slurp away all of your funds. Also of note are the chocolate XLB, which sound gimmicky but are marvelous little pouches filled with chocolate and banana. This is one of the more full-service, modern places on the crawl, so take advantage of the proper bathrooms and napkins.

2 GOLDEN SHOPPING MALL: TIANJIN DUMPLING HOUSE, LAN ZHOU

Steps from the LIRR and subway, **TIANJIN** is the perfect first stop in Flushing, a no-holds-barred introduction to all that is authentic and special about the area. **THE GOLDEN SHOPPING MALL** is a little hard to find, not as well indicated as the New World Mall across the street, so look carefully at the street numbers for a small sign indicating the entrance. This subterranean sea of food stalls is thick with the steam from many kinds of dumplings and noodles boiling, as well as a cacophony of sounds and oil smells, but the winding path to Tianjin Dumpling House is pretty well marked and worth the journey. Seating is limited and not designed for comfort, so try to elbow your way into a spot at the small counter, ideally in front of the proprietary garlic sauce. All of the dumplings are boiled, but the thicker, chewy skin stands up well, offering the sturdiness needed to hold in all the flavors and not disintegrate in the boiling. The item to get here is unconventional: lamb and squash dumplings, which at $5 for a plate of 12 offers more flavor per dollar than most other dishes. The lamb flavor is big; there is a vinegar sauce that provides a nice acid to cut the lamb, and the chili oil is a must-do on everything, as is the garlic sauce for an interesting change. There is a mini buffet of more exotic offerings that most people carry away, but dumplings are the way to go.

3

JOE'S STEAMED RICE ROLLS

Any place with a devotion to a singular dish has a lot of pressure to execute perfectly, and **JOE'S** does not disappoint. A storefront and the only food option in a mini-mall of different vendors (where else can you get a cellphone case, a Korean face mask, and a check cashed?), Joe's turns out the best rice rolls, each element completed by hand, by Joe himself. Joe grinds his own rice for the batter in an electric powered stone mill imported from China, and steams it in twin steamers, each big enough to accommodate a sheet pan. All you have to do is select your filling and vegetables.

The rice rolls are thin and fluffy, a completely different beast from those pale imitations offered at most dim sum restaurants, and you can taste every ingredient. This is the way to experience what an authentic rice roll is all about. N.B.: Chef's favorite combination is beef and egg.

4 WHITE BEAR

WHITE BEAR has been discovered by camera-wielding foodies, much to the annoyance of the proprietors, who do not want to be photographed, a virtually impossible feat given the Lilliputian size of the place. Don't fret, dear owners, the real star here is the dumplings, especially the number six, "wontons in chili oil." The chili oil delivers more funky flavor than true spicy heat, and the pork and veggie dumplings are light and tasty. No matter how full you are a plate of these dumplings somehow disappears really easily. They also offer a variety of frozen dumplings if you would like to try to replicate the experience at home, but without the proper chili oil and glaring owners it most likely won't be the same.

5 SZECHUAN HOUSE

By this time it is expected that you are tired and ready for a proper seat and a proper glass of wine. Both, as well as some remarkable *mapo* tofu, *dan dan* noodles, and other Szechuan specialties can be found at **SZECHUAN HOUSE**, which has been operating for 33 years. Szechuan House has tablecloths, silverware, and an attentive waitstaff, which feels downright luxurious after the cramped quarters and thin paper napkins of some of the dumpling places. The Szechuan dishes are all spot-on in flavor, and devoid of any grease. The aforementioned mapo tofu is silken and well rounded, putting many other versions of this dish to shame and should not be missed. Szechuan House is also close to the 7 train, making it the perfect way to unwind before you head back to Manhattan, full of warm tea and hot spice.

Bonus Crawls

Gowanus, Brooklyn

THE GOWANUS CANAL has not always had the best reputation, but it's cleaning up its act, literally; designated as an EPA Superfund cleanup site in 2009, the canal was rezoned to allow for residential buildings. The reported onetime mob dumping ground and home to three-eyed fish is now a scenic spot in the middle of Brooklyn, and many restaurants are taking advantage of the water views. The many warehouses give the neighborhood an industrial feel, and there are pockets of side streets with local artists and businesses, but it is still a bit rough. Gowanus is an adventure that pays off in food and fun.

AMPLE HILLS

This playful ice cream spot has a down-home feel, and they churn out rich creamy ice cream with lots of fun and surprising mix-ins (peppermint patties, brownies, munchie mix, etc). Fun fact: They pasteurize on site, thus making them a registered dairy plant. Grab your ice cream and head upstairs for seats facing the canal and the New York City skyline.
305 NEVINS ST., BROOKLYN,
(347) 725-4061, AMPLEHILLS.COM

INSA

Delicious, high quality Korean BBQ set on an industrial street near the Gowanus canal. After feasting, head into one of five uniquely themed karaoke rooms, or the retro bar with fish tanks and creative cocktails up front.
328 DOUGLASS ST., BROOKLYN, (718) 855-2620, INSABROOKLYN.COM

PIG BEACH

An indoor/outdoor beer garden set above the canal, **PIG BEACH** features some of the most exciting BBQ and all-around cheat day food. Bring your dogs, babies, and a group of friends to eat and drink away a beautiful day at this sprawling outdoor spot.

48 UNION ST.; (718)737-7181; WWW.PIGBEACHNYC.COM

ROYAL PALMS SHUFFLEBOARD CLUB

Set in a 17,000-square-foot warehouse, **RPSC** is a playground for the over-21 set. One of 10 full-size shuffleboard courts can be rented on a first-come basis. While you're waiting, relax in the retro Floridian setting with tropical drinks, board games (regular and oversize), feast on fare from rotating local food trucks, or dance to the DJs spinning tunes. It is a wonderland of kitsch, with booze.

514 UNION ST., BROOKLYN, (347) 223-4410, ROYALPALMSSHUFFLE.COM

Staten Island

WHOEVER SAID LIFE IS A JOURNEY NOT A DESTINATION must have been on the Staten Island Ferry. A free ride from NYC to Staten Island, the ferry is a way to take in the fantastic views and some fresh(ish) air. Here are a few gems to check out across the harbor.

BAYOU

Creole style at its best!

1072 BAY ST., STATEN ISLAND, (718) 273-4383, BAYOUNYC.COM

BLUE

What's the point of being on an island if you can't see the water? This is the waterfront seafood restaurant to hit on Staten Island.

1115 RICHMOND TER., STATEN ISLAND, (718) 273-7777, BLUERESTAURANTNYC.COM

ENOTECA MARIA

The kitchen is manned by a rotating staff of nonnas (grandmothers). They cook according to their region, and the menu changes accordingly. Cash only.

27 HYATT ST., STATEN ISLAND, (718)447-2777, ENOTECAMARIA.COM

LAKRUWANA

Famous, over-the-top weekend buffet and elaborate decor. The Sri Lankan cuisine is well worth the trip.

668 BAY STREET, STATEN ISLAND, (347) 857-8869, LAKRUWANA.COM

Eateries by Cuisine & Specialty

French

Balthazar, 99
db bistro moderne, 33
Eleven Madison Park, 43
Le CouCou, 100
Minetta Tavern, 59
Raoul's, 101

Hot Dogs

Gray's Papaya, 14

Italian

Barbuto, 91
Bar Pitti, 58
Casa Lever, 26
Cecconi's, 151
Enoteca Maria, 192
Enzo's, 178
Faicco's Italian Specialties, 85
Fred's at Barneys Madison
   Avenue, 3
L'Artusi, 80
Lilia, 142
Locanda Verde, 126
Supper, 70
Tra di Noi, 183

Jewish

Bubby's, 123
Katz's Delicatessen, 117
Russ & Daughters Cafe, 116

Mediterranean

Amaranth, 2

Middle Eastern

Mamoun's, 60

Moroccan

Café Mogador, 66

Noodles

Great New York Noodletown, 108
Ippudo Westside, 31
Lam Zhou Handmade Noodle, 107
Momofuku Noodle Bar, 67
TsuruTonTan, 51
Xi'an Famous Foods, 68

Pizza

Adrienne's Pizza Bar, 132
Emmy Squared, 140
Joe's, 87
John's of Bleecker, 84

Seafood

Blue, 193
Brooklyn Crab, 167
Grand Banks, 124
Luke's Lobster, 150
Lure, 103
Maison Premiere, 145
Mary's Fish Camp, 77
Randazzo's, 179

Southern

Commodore, The, 144
Sylvia's, 158

Spanish

Casa Mono, 54
El Quinto Pino, 93

Steakhouse

Delmonico's, 131
Peter Luger Steakhouse, 139

Index

Photo Credits

Pg. iii © istock.com/TraceRouda
Pg. iv (top) © Oleg March
Pg. iv (bottom) © Jen Balisi, @indulgenteats
Pg. v (bottom) © Alexa Mehraban, @eatingnyc
Pg. vi © istock.com/spyarm
Pg. 6 © Photos taken by Margarita Ma Garcia Acevedo for EAT
Pg. 7 © Serendipity 3
Pg. 10, 11 Alexandra Romanoff, @onemoredish
g. 15 © Alexa Mehraban, @eatingnyc
Pg. 18 (top) © Daniel Krieger
Pg. 18 (bottom) © Jen Balisi, @indulgenteats
Pg. 24, 25 © Alexandra Romanoff, @onemoredish
Pg. 26, 27 (top) © Henry Hargreaves
Pg. 27 (bottom) © You Jean Han
Pg. 31 © Alexa Mehraban @eatingnyc
Pg. 33 (top) © Alexandra Romanoff, @OneMoreDish
Pg. 35 © Jean Lee, @jeaniuseats
Pg. 38 © Ellen Silverman
Pg. 39 (top) © Maura McEvoy
Pg. 41 © Jen Balisi, @indulgenteats
Pg. 42 (top) © Rockwell Group, Emily Andrews
Pg. 42 (bottom) © Liz Clayman
Pg. 48, 49 (top) © Black Paw Photography.
Pg. 49 (bottom) © Alexa Mehraban, @eatingnyc
Pg. 59 © Emilie Baltz
Pg. 62 © Gotham Bar & Grill
Pg. 70 © Supper
Pg. 71, 72 © Angel's Share
Pg. 78-79 © Henry Hargreaves for Bar Sardine
Pg. 85 © Alexa Mehraban, @eatinging
Pg. 90 © Jen Balisi, @indulgenteasts
Pg. 91 (bottom) © Alexandra Romanoff, @onemoredish
Pg. 94 © The Red Cat NYC
Pg. 95 © Gigi Altarejos
Pg. 100 © Corry Arnold
Pg. 101 © Jen Balisi, @indulgenteats
Pg. 103 © Jackie Gebel, @noleftovers
Pg. 109 © Barbara Leung
Pg. 117 © Alexa Mehraban, @eatingnyc
Pg. 122, 123 (top) © Jen Balisi, @indulgenteats

About The Authors

SISTERS DARYL ZWEBEN HOM AND ALI ZWEBEN IMBER are fourth generation in the hospitality business. Both graduates of the prestigious Cornell School of Hotel Administration, Ali and Daryl started their blog, the *Sisterhood of the Unbuttoning Pants*, after many requests from friends for restaurant recommendations. Both sisters have relevant and varied work experiences in hospitality, PR, and marketing, which contribute to their knowledge and love of the food world. Their unique voice and on-point reviews have gained them a massive following and secured them as a go-to-resource for all things dining in New York.

Pg. 124 (top) © Alan Silverman
Pg. 124 (bottom) © Alexander Pincus
Pg. 125 (top left) © Grand Banks
Pg. 125 (top right, bottom) Alexander Pincus
Pg. 126 © Jen Balisi, @indulgenteats
Pg. 127 © Brandy Library
Pg. 130, 131 © Delmonico's Restaurant
Pg. 133 © Eric Laignel
Pg. 134 (top) © Henry Hargreaves
Pg. 135 © Bjorn Wallander
Pg. 138 photo by Eric Isaac
Pg. 142, 143 © Evan Sung
Pg. 144 © Mouthfeel Magazine
Pg. 145-147 © Maison Premiere
Pg. 150 © Luke's Lobster
Pg. 151 © Jackie Gebel, @noleftovers
Pg. 152, 153 © River Cafe
Pg. 154, 155 © James Baigrie
Pg. 159 © Marcus Samuelsson Group
Pg. 161 (top) © Brent Herrig
Pg. 161 (bottom) © Daniel Kreiger
Pg. 167 © Brooklyn Crab
Pg. 170 © istock.com/delray77
Pg. 172 (top) © Virginia Rollison
Pg. 172 (bottom) © Evan Sung
Pg. 173 (top) © Virginia Rollison
Pg. 173 (bottom) © Evan Joseph
Pg. 174, 175 © Le District
Pg. 189 © Alexa Mehraban, @eatingnyc
Pg. 190 © Jean Lee, @jeaniuseats
Pg. 192 © Jackie Gebel, @noleftovers
Pg. 193 © istock.com/AJDepew

All other photos © The Sisterhood of the Unbuttoning Pants